I'VE TRIED
EVERYTHING
&
NOTHING
WORKS

RESOURCE GUIDE

A.J. MCMAHAN

CONTENTS

OUR GREATEST RESOURCE

First, God is our greatest resource. The next greatest resource you have at your disposal is you. I will add information that has been extremely helpful to other caregivers in determining the Most Effective strategies to help their children succeed. Each resource has come from tried and tested methods used by caregivers themselves. The information is also kid-friendly. What I mean is, each resource helps children from their perspective. Nothing in this library will crush your child's spirit, make him feel controlled or stifle his development. Everything in this Resource Guide, when used appropriately, is effective for helping children thrive.

My toddler son likes to play with bath toys. One of his favorites is a plastic scoop with slits in the bottom that allow water to strain through. He has fun with it, except when he is trying to capture water to pour over his head. The scoop captures water, but almost all of the water is gone by the time he raises the scoop to his head. At first, he was frustrated, not understanding why he couldn't effectively pour water over his head despite his intense and repeated efforts.

Most of you have been discouraged by your attempts to help your child change. Your intense efforts have seemed to yield some success at times, but any progress seems to drain out with your goals left unaccomplished. The intensity of problems your child is having and the accompanying pressures creates desperation for change in many of you. Desperation cannot be the drive for your process.

If necessity is the mother of creation, then desperation is its father. If you allow desperation, fear, guilt, or anything other than faith and works to drive your process, you will likely remain stuck in draining efforts that produce few results. Using a personalized L.E.A.P. process avoids that trap, as it is a comprehensive strategy you prepare before implementation that is focused on equipping and empowering your child to transform in a specific, measurable way.

Change is improvement in your child's behavior. Change is displayed externally. Change can happen quickly, but often doesn't last. Transformation is improvement in your child's strength of character and belief in himself. This occurs internally. Transformation lasts because your child grows strong enough internally to maintain the change.

A new discipline strategy can promote your child's behavior to change. Change in your child's behavior can also result from counseling for your child, focused on the therapist being the primary promotor of change. Change can result from reward systems and medication. While these methods promote change, they often fall short on promoting transformation—which is your child developing enough internal strength of mind, emotion and character to maintain the change for good.

Your child is beyond tips and tricks or a new or specific discipline strategy. The depth of your child's internal challenge with her impulses has been reinforced by days, weeks and maybe years of repeating the same maladaptive behavior. Your child has experienced and is experiencing hidden rewards from the emotional and behavioral problems she is displaying.

Your child is in a valley of behavior where he is comfortable. Now you are telling your child to push a character boulder up a large hill of change because life is so much better on the other side. And your child is thinking, *Yeah, right!* Your child doesn't believe that because he hasn't experienced success on the other side of the hill. Your child's current experiences from the maladaptive behavior are experientially sweet to him. The way to success is to equip and empower your child to stop pouring energy into sabotaging your efforts at change due to familiarity and comfort at the deepest levels, and to channel that energy into pushing himself towards transformation.

This work can and will happen when you bring all the resources God has given you to bear into a comprehensive strategy to equip and empower your child to transform. L.E.A.P. is a solid foundation for transformation. We do not live on solid foundations alone. We build on solid foundations and live in further developed constructions. This Resource Guide is designed to help you construct an effective Plan supporting your L.E.A.P. process and particularly your ability to implement Affirming Accountability.

A comprehensive strategy is what I refer to as your "Plan." Empowering your child to transform will not thrive on a foundation alone. I want you and your child to succeed. Despite all you've been through, there is a greater chance of success when you bring all the tools and resources you believe will be effective to bear to help your child overcome internal challenges. Your child's problems are not your fault. You are, however, in the perfect position to equip and empower your child to transform.

Adamantly refuse to use this Resource Guide to find the "right" discipline strategy in certain situations. God has put you in a position to equip and empower your child. This Resource Guide is here to help equip and empower you. Use it to formulate a comprehensive strategy that is powerful and effective in motivating your child to transform.

Belief is powerful. Routines are powerful. Affirmation built on the foundation of a loving relationship is powerful. Challenging your child to stretch to reach a new height in ability based on your belief in her is powerful. Consistency is powerful. Overcoming your own emotional and relational obstacles is powerful. Putting all these together will push you from 70-80% of the Most Effective Actions to the 97% to 98% range on a daily basis to help your child succeed. Don't settle for less than creating a comprehensive Plan, then implement it with Perseverance. You and your child will succeed.

This resource guide is a library of information from which you can pick and choose what will be Most Effective for your child when implementing Affirming Accountability. Seek insight (without negative judgment) into your needs in your process and the needs of your child. Even if you don't know the child in your care very well, if you are the primary caregiver, you likely know the child better than just about anyone else.

I've never seen caregivers who try to take shortcuts succeed in helping their child transform. Conversely, I've never seen caregivers who have put the time in on the front end to examine each L.E.A.P. principle, develop them to fit their child, and develop a comprehensive Plan to support their process not achieve life-altering results. Prepare to equip and empower your child to transform with these five steps:

1. Believe your child is capable.
2. Before changing anything, write and review each L.E.A.P. step to ensure strength in that area.
3. Use the Resource Guide to create a comprehensive Plan to support Affirming Accountability and avoid anything that might sabotage your efforts.
4. Then, and only then, sit down with your child and communicate briefly your Expectation of Excellence. Communicate your belief in your child's ability. Explain that you will hold your child accountable. (You don't have to explain how; just say, "You won't like the consequences.")
5. Implement your Plan with conviction and consistency. Persevere until your child transforms.

You and your child can do this. You are meant to. I believe in God and I believe in you and your child.

TRUST YOURSELF

Many caregivers ask me, "AJ, what about this or that as a part of my Plan?" Let me give an example from one mom who had a question for me while constructing her Plan. "As a part of my Plan, I want to pick a time each day to review my specific Expectation of Excellence (an essential element of the L.E.A.P. process) with my kids, a time of calm. What do you think about that, AJ?"

"Sure, go ahead," I replied. "The important thing is that your Plan consists of what you really believe in. If you truly believe something will be helpful for your child, do it. If you personally don't believe in something, I don't care what the experts say, including me, don't do it." You must use your own ingenuity to develop your Plan.

One dad and mom created a system by which they equated their Affirming Accountability to coins. What was most important to their daughter was time on her tablet. They chose a number of coins, three, to represent ten-minute increments of tablet time each. When their daughter did not meet their specific Expectation—"You will handle all upsetting situations without an outburst"—with Excellence, they took a coin. It's not that their daughter couldn't cry when upset about something in her life. This Expectation of Excellence was understood between their seven-year-old and them to mean the hour-long, nonstop, frequent meltdowns when she didn't get her way. Those had to stop.

The caregivers came up with the coin idea themselves. I didn't like it at first because it seemed too close to a reward system, which has little to no effectiveness long-term with children who primarily operate in line with the strong-willed temperament. The cool thing was, it was a choice-and-consequence system, but the caregivers liked the coin as a part of their Plan. I had never used a coin in this way before, nor did I have experience with other caregivers who had. The caregivers of this seven-year-old girl believed in this method, so I gave them the go-ahead. After our discussion, they asked if I thought it was a good idea, and I replied with confidence that it would work. They asked why I was so confident after initially being hesitant, and I replied, "Two reasons. First, it is still built on the foundation of choice and consequence, not reward. Second, you believe in it—so it will definitely will be effective." And it was.

Their seven-year old daughter who had thrown uncontrollable meltdowns for an hour or longer frequently since she was two years old stopped herself the first night they implemented their fully prepared Plan. They told her "no" that evening about something she wanted, and she sucked in a breath in preparation to let the meltdown fly. With the first hint of the impending outburst, her mom stated, "That's a coin." To her parents' absolute shock and amazement, their daughter cut off her emotion-fueled tantrum instantaneously, grabbed a pillow, and for the first time they had ever seen, controlled herself despite her emotions. Keep in mind that this, just like your story, was just the beginning. Her caregivers had to Persevere for months, remaining consistent through their child's rough patches until she built the internal strength necessary to control herself consistently.

As you examine some of the following methods throughout this Resource Guide to help tweak your Plan to make it the Most Effective it can be, take what you believe will be helpful to you as you construct your comprehensive Plan including L.E.A.P. Also, when you have an idea you believe in, add that. You are the expert on your child. Don't let your mom, neighbors, the school or anyone stop you from doing what you believe will be the Most Effective in helping your child succeed. As long as it's done in the true light of love, with God's true approval, not a man-made twist, go for it. I hope the following Resources are of great help to you. I believe they will be.

OUTWIT, OUTLAST, OUTPLAY

Survivor first aired May 31, 2000, as an American reality TV series. Contestants had to weather extreme challenges while "Outwitting, Outlasting and Outplaying" every other contestant. You are now in the family version of *Survivor*. Congratulations!

Outwit your child with Godly wisdom. Plan proactively and face your fear of your worst-case scenario.

Outlast your child by Persevering until your child meets your Expectation of Excellence, showing himself that he can do it.

Outplay means you are capable. God would not have entrusted the child in your care to you if you weren't capable of equipping and empowering your child to succeed. Use the tools and resources God has given you to implement a comprehensive Plan you believe in to Outplay your way to success.

There was only one winner in each season of *Survivor*. The cool thing about the family version is that when you win...your child, your family, and your hopes win! Prepare your Plan to guide you to Outwit, Outlast and Outplay your child daily. Empower your child to experience futility in trying to work against, around, under, over or through you. Help your child experience that the only path to success is *with* you. Once you convince your child of this through love, your child will stop pouring his energy into fighting against you and will instead pour energy into fighting to overcome his problems and impulses.

RESPONSIBILITY

This section has one of the most important concepts to employ as you implement your Plan. Let's call it "what goes on the table, stays on the table." Your child will overcome the main concerns you have by learning to meet your Expectation with Excellence one at a time. Hold your child responsible to your Expectation above everything non-essential.

Responsibility to meet your Expectation with Excellence is prioritized above everything, save God and essential needs. Say your Expectation is for your child to do what you've told them right away, like Chastity's caregivers. Once Chastity's grandparents implemented their fully prepared Plan, when Chastity didn't go brush her teeth right away when her grandfather told her, she had electronics taken away for an effective length of time. This consequence appropriately reinforced the Expectation; however, Chastity was still responsible for obeying the original polite command of "Go brush your teeth." Obeying the command remains Chastity's responsibility, i.e. "on the table" until Chastity follows through with Excellence.

Once a responsibility for your child is on the table, it stays on the table. Your child is responsible for removing the obstacle standing in the way of what's important *to* them. Chastity, for example, may have had her electronics taken for an hour because she didn't comply, yet the Expectation of "do what we tell you to do right away," i.e. brush your teeth, is still her responsibility. Chastity must understand that the responsibility of obedience is prioritized above anything else save sleep, food, attending school if applicable and anything else absolutely essential to life. Everything else she'd like to do is on hold until she complies. All "extras" are suspended until Chastity takes care of her responsibility.

Chastity's opportunity to learn that she is responsible for her choices is reinforced by this process. If she chooses not to brush her teeth, the extra time she loses from enjoying her privileges is also on her. She might go to bed and to school without her teeth brushed. This might be embarrassing to caregivers, yet Chastity's caregivers kept their eyes focused on their hope for their granddaughter, to become a responsible person. Chastity's grandparents held this hope paramount to embarrassment, their fears, what other people might think and anything else that might try to hinder the essential life skills they were helping their granddaughter build.

Chastity couldn't do anything non-essential until she complied. Her grandparents learned not to argue, plead or engage. Just to simply and consistently enforce. They had to outlast Chastity until she got tired of not getting to do anything she wanted to do or have anything she wanted to have like dessert after dinner. Ultimately, she got tired of not being able to enjoy her privileges and asked, "What do I need to do?" Her caregiver remained steadfast and asked her calmly and firmly, "What did I tell you to do?" They held Chastity responsible for remembering that she needed to brush her teeth and then do it.

Jasmine's specific Expectation was, "Jasmine, you will not throw any tantrums at school." When Jasmine threw a tantrum at school, she would receive a firm and appropriate spanking at home. Let's say that Jasmine's mom reviewed the daily report from school indicating Jasmine threw a tantrum in school that day. After a brief discussion about this, Jasmine's mom told Jasmine to go to her room to receive her spanking. Let's say that Jasmine ran away from her. Jasmine's mom would not chase, plead, yell or demand that Jasmine go to her room. She would go about her life. Now, "Go in your room and receive the consequence of your actions," i.e. the firm and appropriate spanking, is on the table. Everything that is nonessential for Jasmine is on hold until she complies.

Jasmine's mom's responsibility is to calmly monitor what Jasmine does. If Jasmine tries to play with toys or electronics, watch television, or do anything nonessential, her mom is to stop her until she complies with her firm and appropriate spanking. Wisely, Jasmine's mom will avoid this becoming a power struggle. If it takes methodically removing items from reach or the house to enforce this boundary, her mom would do so. Jasmine's mom might also communicate that the longer Jasmine takes to comply, this might result in further loss of privileges after she complies with her spanking. Jasmine will know that what she is missing out on is a result of her choice to disobey her mom in the midst of the process of Affirming Accountability. Jasmine ultimately must choose to take responsibility for her choice to throw a tantrum in school, including her response to the firm and appropriate consequence of a spanking, in order to move beyond to what she enjoys.

Bill was aggressive with his mom. After she implemented her Plan to stop his aggression towards her, he began kicking holes in walls. None of us want to experience our child being destructive like that. Some of you caregivers will have a child that will try to terrorize you into giving up when holding them Accountable. They will threaten some of your greatest fears including hurting themselves, running away, being aggressive, super intense outbursts and/or destroying things. Intervene with support when you know there is true danger for yourself and others. No matter what, remain resolved in the midst of the threat. If your child threatens to kill himself, take him to the hospital. If he threatens to hurt others, make sure they are protected. If your child is prone to destroying things, the work to repair or pay for the damage by doing age-appropriate tasks as restitution will be on the table until he meets this responsibility. When you know to what extremes your child may go to try to intimidate you, explain to your child up front what will happen if he makes any of these choices. If your child catches you off guard, it is *still fair* to hold him accountable afterward for impulsive and unhealthy reactions to your Affirming Accountability.

No matter what, when implementing your Plan, when something goes on the table, it is your child who must remove it from the table. Your job is not to try to force your child to make a good choice or accept the consequences afterward. Your job is to respect your child's choices and enforce the responsibility for that choice landing squarely on your child's shoulders every single time. Remember, consequences are not negative. Consequences are simply the outcome of choices. Consequences for good choices equal appropriate access to the activities and privileges you want your child to enjoy.

RESPONSIBILITY SABOTEURS

Three great saboteurs to helping our children develop the character strength of responsibility are reminding, rewarding, and repeating. Many caregivers are using these strategies in their efforts to help their children become responsible when, in fact, these three crafty influences undermine their efforts.

Reminding

You want Johnny to remember to brush his teeth in the morning. Every morning you remind Johnny to brush his teeth. You feel that it is essential to remind Johnny because, if you don't, he will likely not brush his teeth. Who is taking ownership for remembering the importance of Johnny's teeth being brushed? I hear caregivers respond, "I know, but if I don't remind him, he won't do it." Reminding teaches our children ages 4-5 and up dependence, not responsibility. We are instilling in our children a belief that we don't truly believe they will do it on their own, so we must prompt them. Reminding tacitly communicates to children that we do not believe they can or will remember.

We take responsibility when we remind our children. Children operating with the strong-willed temperament welcome leaning on us instead of leaning on themselves to take responsibility. If you want your child to take responsibility fully, you must give her responsibility fully. To whatever degree we take responsibility, we concurrently take away a child's opportunity to be responsible, while unintentionally sowing seeds of dependence.

You must Plan courageously to allow the full weight of appropriate responsibility to fall squarely on your child's shoulders, not yours. This means you don't remind. As part of your Plan, create a routine, a process that repeatedly teaches specific actions. Implement the routine, and then put positive pressure on your child to remember by connecting what's important _to_ your child to what's important _for_ your child. For example, no video games that evening if the three specific "get ready" goals are not met in the morning. Examples of three specific "get ready" goals are: 1. Brush your teeth; 2. Be fully dressed with shoes on; 3. Be at the door with your backpack on by 6:45 a.m. Another example might be: 1. Have your clothes on, breakfast eaten, and the dog fed by 6:30 a.m.

Forget about charts. Work with your child incrementally, systematically, to follow the routine you prepare. Plan the routine and all significant elements thoroughly. Take into account everything you need to set up your process for success. No shortcuts. What time do you need to get up to be successful? What will be the best time to review your child's progress and implement accountability if necessary? Have you made your action expectations for your child concrete and measurable with a yes or no? Have you kept the specific action steps your child must take to three or less? What do you need to be consistent?

Once you've thoroughly Planned the routine your child will be Expected to follow with Excellence, explain the routine to your child. Be brief and specific. Then implement the routine. Repetition and consistency are the keys. Use the same process and the same words each day. Review with your child each evening specifically how they did with the routine that day. Affirm what they did well and reinforce what they need to change the next day to meet the Expectation of the routine with Excellence.

During the first week or two, just focus on training her to complete the routine as if she's never done it before. When you reach the point during the first one to two weeks of training that you are fairly confident your child knows what she is expected to do, as you expect her to do it, then start holding her accountable. When she doesn't put forth the effort to remember, it must cost her. Your consistent routine and daily Affirming Accountability will equip and empower your child to remember.

Some of you do not need a comprehensive process; you only need the courage to know your child is capable of remembering. When children are old enough and able to remember other life factors that are important to them, this is evidence that they are capable of remembering...your child is likely just not motivated to remember. Connect what's important *to* your child with what's important *for* him to remember. Use the principles in the book and resource guide to your advantage, and you will be courageously choosing the Most Effective Actions to empower your child to find a way to remember.

Rewarding

The belief that children need rewards in order to be successful is becoming ubiquitous in our culture, especially as rewards become a shiny yet largely ineffective substitute for lovingly firm discipline. In our schools, our children are often rewarded with treats to motivate them to do what they need to do. I'm not faulting the schools or teachers. Teachers and others often need the rewards because they are not in a position to discipline children the way we as caregivers are.

Discipline means to teach. We are responsible for the task of lovingly teaching our children every day. We must see each opportunity with our children as a chance to pull from our wisdom, maturity, courage, and devotion to teach or allow them to learn naturally imperative and often difficult lessons. We must be willing to give them hard consequences without ever crossing the line of harshness. There is a great difference between firm and fierce, hard and harsh, painful and harmful. True discipline carries all of the former terms and none of the latter. Abuse, however, carries all of the latter and more.

Many caregivers are encouraged to use charts and rewards with children that often have only slight long-term probabilities of success. For many children, the weight of their impulses in the moments of challenge and the potential for the hidden rewards they experience from their choices are more powerful than the hope of the reward that is being offered. I wish reward charts worked well for children operating with the strong-willed temperament, but these external motivators are not more powerful than the child's internal struggles and motivators.

When we discuss rewarding, we are not talking about positive praise, affirmation, affection, and relational bonds, which children should be given regularly in healthy measure according to their individual needs. These are, in fact, the most important and powerful rewards. Our children can internalize these rewards. It makes sense to cultivate the seeds of internal rewards as this is the rich soil in which personal responsibility takes root.

Rewarding can be used as a tool when your child achieves something extraordinary. Rewarding just cannot be a foundational element for change. Your 12 and under, choice-and-consequence learner needs Love and Affirming Accountability as the foundation of change, because this is effective where they are developmentally. If they behave above and beyond, it's acceptable to reward them or you can use rewards as an icing-on-the-cake supplement. As long as you don't try to encourage your child to transform on the foundation of external rewards, the method will be effective.

Repeating

In the midst of the struggle, many caregivers find themselves giving the same command or ultimatum five to ten times or more. Caregivers often feel the sting of regret for repeating, yet feel helpless to enact any other process, as "remaining calm" has been futile in getting their children to listen.

Caregivers would like to tell their children one time to do something, without threatening consequences, and have them respond immediately and with an appropriate attitude; however, these types of responses become more akin to the miraculous than the mundane. Caregivers find themselves repeating, and ultimately yelling, as the only source of motivating the children to ultimately and frantically do what they need them to do.

The golden rule for children two or three and older is to not repeat your polite command more than twice, then act. This requires specifically planning and training our children with the L.E.A.P. steps to do what we tell them the first time. Believe it or not, this can happen. I'll elaborate on this as we discuss how to turn the tables on reminding, rewarding and repeating to move you into the 97% to 98% range of effectiveness in empowering your child.

Turning the Tables on Reminding, Rewarding & Repeating

Let's examine how to use reminding, rewarding, and repeating in our efforts to help our children develop responsibility. You may be confused at this moment, because I indicated that reminding, rewarding, and repeating are great saboteurs to responsibility; however, we can use them to aid efforts instead of undermine them.

Reminding. Develop a system in which your child must pay attention to and therefore remind himself of what he needs to do. You accomplish this by firmly putting the responsibility for remembering on his shoulders. You must become excellent at understanding the truth of responsibility—what is your responsibility and what is your child's. You must courageously go through the pain of your child embracing responsibility for his own choices rather than being concerned with how people may judge you. When your child goes to school without his teeth brushed or with messy clothes, people will want to blame you, therefore putting the responsibility on you for the condition of your child. Have you done something wrong? Is there something that you have neglected to do that has caused this outcome? Is your child in any immediate harm because his teeth are not brushed? Is it more important for your child to go to school every day with immaculately brushed teeth or to slowly develop the ability to take ownership of brushing his teeth for himself?

Focus on the responsibility itself while placing it squarely where it belongs. Our responsibility to our children is to train them, and their responsibility is to respond with actions that support their character growth. When our children choose not to accept our teaching, it is up to us to be patient with them, while it is up to them to be fully responsible for the choice they are making. We empower this by not taking the responsibility on ourselves because of guilt, embarrassment, or by doing for them what they need to do for themselves.

We incorporate in our process that our child remembers and reminds himself. Use routines, give him the tools, take the first week or two to go over the process with your child to ensure he knows exactly what's expected. In this process, get to a point where you are confident he understands and is capable. Then hold him accountable. If he forgets, he is accountable. If he chooses not to, he is accountable. When people try to hold you accountable for your child's choices, hold firm to your Plan and the truth of where the responsibility truly rests. Reminding is us taking responsibility repeatedly. What we must do instead is act so that we teach and expect our children, fairly and firmly, to remind themselves.

Rewarding. The biggest rewards for kids are time, attentive affirmation, and confidence that comes from them experiencing personal success over their impulses. Even amidst the busyness of life, our child needs undivided attention. Zig Ziglar said, "How do kids spell love? T-I-M-E." Ask yourself how you're doing at giving your child needed time and attention. When you have a positive answer, great. If you don't, what can you do to improve? Start with small increments of focused time and attention if necessary. At one point, realizing I was not doing well with this, I started with one minute of undivided attention to each child per night. This was a manageable improvement to start with that stretched me and improved my relationships with my children. Better to take a baby step and build on it consistently than a bigger step that is difficult to commit to or follow through on.

Let's be attentive to affirm our child's improvement. Some children don't respond well to verbal affirmation, but most do. Catch your child doing well and praise her. Recognize the improvements specifically when you discuss with your child how she did at meeting your Expectation of Excellence that day. Sometimes when you see your child wrestling with the decision in the moment, say, "I see you are struggling, and I know you can do it. Make yourself proud." Even if she doesn't make the right decision, affirm that you saw her wrestling within herself to try to make the right choice. Hopefully, she will next time.

When your 12 and under, choice-and-consequence learner is receiving effective empowerment consistently from you, she will have the needed support to win the inner battle more often. The more your child redirects her energy into positive choices, the more confidence she will gain in her ability to overcome her impulses. Your child will feel great about her choices and therefore herself. This will empower a reinforcement cycle of your child seeking to feel good not by giving in to the momentary impulses, but by enjoying the victory of pushing herself to a higher level of improvement. This inner victory is one of the greatest rewards we can empower our children to experience.

We can use external rewards for extraordinary efforts and icing-on-the-cake type encouragement; however, to empower lasting change, we have to help our children hunger for inner rewards. A healthy amount of regular, focused time with our children, attentive affirmation, and inner happiness and confidence from their own successes over their impulses, empowered by our lovingly firm, consistent Accountability are the Most Effective rewards our child can experience.

Repeating. We will set a standard for ourselves that we will not repeat ourselves. From the age of two or three up, we will tell our children only once or twice what we expect them to do in that moment. This also includes developing and demonstrating a belief that our children are capable of remembering what we tell them to do. In light of this, we will strive to be wise in how many and which tasks we assign at any given time. If your child has trouble doing three consecutive tasks, give two or one. Expect your child to report back to you as part of the process when the task or tasks are complete. This puts the full circle of ownership on her instead of you having to hunt her down. Seek to consistently challenge but not exasperate your child in the number and manner of tasks you assign. She will likely not grow if you do not challenge her to stretch herself. Expect her to remember and follow through.

When I was a child, commercials for a company called E. F. Hutton had a tagline: "When E. F. Hutton speaks, everybody listens." Oh, to be E.F. Hutton! Well we can be E.F. Hutton when we set our minds to it and train our child to respond accordingly. This means that we no longer repeat ourselves beyond saying something twice.

To make the process fair and effective, we ensure from the beginning our child has a clear chance to hear us. This is not necessarily forcing our children to look us directly in the eyes when we speak. Young children often do not, and older children may not, which is normal. We get our child's attention while in his presence—even if he isn't looking at us—then speak in a concise and clear way that he can hear. Once we master this ability to communicate in a way we are sure the child has heard, now our expectation is set for the child to respond to the polite command we have given. This means that the responsibility of attending and acting is on him. And we hold him to this expectation.

When our child chooses not to be responsible with her actions, we hold her Accountable. Instead of reminding and repeating, we ask our child what it was she was supposed to do, helping her understand she is responsible to pay attention to us and remember. We then do not allow her to move forward with any of her personal plans until she remembers and takes care of her responsibilities. This can be arduous work, but if you want your child to learn to treat you like you're E.F. Hutton when you speak, you have to put in the work to make that happen. This comes through consistent, reinforced Expectation with the weight of the lessons applied to our children, and not through weightless words they can easily ignore. You must remain calm, resolute, and firm. Do not waiver in your resolution that your child take her responsibility off the table. All privileges are secondary to the child taking ownership and handling his responsibility. Not with perfection, but with Excellence.

WORST-CASE SCENARIO

" I can't handle that," a mother exclaimed when thinking about the worst-case scenario of how her child might respond when she held her Accountable. But after she had time to reflect on her hopes for her child and Plan how she could put measures in place to effectively deal with her worst-case scenario, she was ready. You are only fully ready with your Plan when you've faced, accepted and planned for your worst-case scenario with your child's reactions and potential life choices.

The action steps needed when facing challenging reactions your child may have are:

- Prevent
- Pretend
- Persevere

Prevent what you can. You are smart. You are capable. What can you do to better set up yourself and your child for success? What works against you? Where are the danger spots? How can you structure a routine or process to eliminate or reduce the likelihood of a trouble spot when holding your child Accountable? What can you remove from the environment?

You cannot control your child. You can control yourself and the elements of your environment. What can you change to empower yourself when working with your child? Some caregivers have to prevent time from working against them. Some have to try to prevent their child from taking out their aggressions on a certain person or in a certain way. Some caregivers have to prevent their own fears or guilt from getting in the way of empowering their child through tough love. Some have to work with their job schedules to prevent problems that arise from not being there enough in order to be effective. Some have to prevent verbal or behavioral undermining from themselves or others. What can you skillfully prevent?

True prevention lessens the struggle. Prevention does not create another situation for you and your child to battle over in the midst of working with your child. Prevention, when done well, doesn't pour gas on the fire. Prevention helps reduce the fire. Do you need to give yourself more time? Remove something from the environment? Avoid inflammatory reactions? What can you do to prevent obstacles while working with your child?

Pretend that the only one who is suffering and will have to answer is your child, and do your best to make it so. Persevere through the pain of your child choosing to make poor decisions until your child surrenders to your love and what's healthy. You may have to prepare supplies for the holes your child will need to patch before any of his privileges are restored. You may have to stand before your child in the most deliberate, not-backing-down, nonaggressive stance you can while looking your child in the eye and saying with smoldering intensity, "Hit me, and you will regret it." (Of course, your response would never be physically aggressive in turn if it came to that, but you must hold your child Accountable in the firmest, most healthy ways you know how.)

It's not a sign of weakness to be afraid of your child or what your child might do. I have been similarly afraid at times. The key is not to show it. Act with courage and love to do what you need to do to empower your child. This is not "pretending," but a higher form of powerfully communicating your strength, love and authority regardless of how you feel. You can do it!

Persevere. You can do all things through Christ who gives you strength (Phil 4:13). Don't bluff. Prepare to act when your child reacts. Be angry and sin not (Ephesians 4:26). Do not take out your anger on your child. Accept your fear, but do not give in to it. Stand firm in the fight against the wrong, not against your child, until your child comes to his senses and surrenders.

In the midst of the battle to help your child overcome a main concern, you will make hard choices in love with your God-given wisdom and strength. The Holy Spirit will guide you. Resolve to stand.

> *Finally, be strong in the Lord and in his mighty power. Put on the full armor of God, so that you can take your stand against the devil's schemes. For our struggle is not against flesh and blood, but against the rulers, against the authorities, against the powers of this dark world and against the spiritual forces of evil in the heavenly realms.*
>
> —Ephesians 6: 10-11

I find it interesting that these verses are in the same chapter as the verse, *"Children, obey your parents in the Lord, for this is right"* (Ephesians 6:1).

What is your worst-case scenario? Write it down. Pray earnestly for the strength not to give in to the fear of it. Give it to God. Face it. Prevent. Pretend. Persevere. This is what is best for you and your child. Even if your child makes the choice to live out your worst-case scenario, at least you did not enable her to welcome doom into her life slowly and perniciously. When you are at the crossroad of acting in line with either hope or fear with your child, choose wisely.

MAKING TIME-OUT EFFECTIVE

Everything in this section will help you tweak your Plan to make a time-out effective.

Effective Time-outs

When: You have time to see it through

Where: Chair without distractions or child's bedroom

Why: Time to think; time to practice self-control; a form of discipline

How: The key is first to train your child to participate in a time-out appropriately. When balancing training your child to participate in a time-out appropriately versus the amount of time, prioritize the training. For example, the suggested guideline for a time-out for young children is one minute per year of age; however, if you are working with a child that has not done a time-out according to your expectations, trying to have a six-year-old sit quietly in time-out for six minutes may not be the Most Effective. Prioritize what you are training and use time judiciously. For example, you want to train your child to participate in a time-out as you expect. Set two or three specific, measurable rules for a time-out that covers what you expect your child to do during a time-out. For example, your two or three time-out rules might be something like these:

1. You will keep your bottom on the seat/floor.
2. You must be quiet the entire time. No screaming or yelling.
3. Your time will start when your bottom is on the seat/floor and you are quiet. The time will start over if your bottom is not on the seat/floor or you scream or yell.

If your child has to keep his bottom on the seat/floor, he cannot get up, run around or stand up and accomplish this requirement. When your child is "quiet," you can permit reasonable noise such as crying softly or sniffling, but they are not talking, screaming, crying, whining or calling your name 50 times. Set one to three measurable rules that simply and effectively encompass your expectations. You may have to give this some thought. Use your own ingenuity. When you start training your child to participate in a time-out as you expect, set what you feel is an effective amount of time for your child to start with. This amount of time is just enough to require your child to push himself to practice self-control, but also a reasonable amount of time so that you can start the timer over repeatedly, as it may take your child several efforts to be trained.

At first, you might find it reasonable to require your child to complete one full minute of sitting with her bottom in the chair while being reasonably quiet, regardless of age. This is because you will hold your child accountable to meeting this expectation. When your child tests the boundaries, i.e. gets up, her time starts over. When she makes a noise, other than an arbitrary cough or other reasonable noise, her time starts over. This could go on for a while until your child completes the full amount of time exactly as you expect. Starting with just 30 seconds at first is acceptable as long as it is an increment of time that will challenge your child. Your child's time will not start until she is meeting the clearly communicated rules. Your child will learn that you truly hold her accountable to your expectations and that she must master herself in order to move forward.

Do not chase your child or beg him to complete the time-out. Do not remind him. Simply go about your life. Meet all your child's needs while suspending all wants with gravitas. When your child asks you about dessert, going outside, the tablet, etc. respond with something like, "I will not consider allowing you a privilege until you do what you need to do. What do you need to do?" Time-out is now "on the table." Hold your child accountable. Don't equivocate. Avoid over helping. Allow your child to struggle to remember, take you seriously, and meet your Expectation with Excellence. Just like on *Survivor,* outlast your child until he surrenders and complies fully with the time-out as needed. Once your child has mastered the first measure of time, thirty seconds to one minute as in our example, then increase the time gradually until your child can master the full amount of time you think appropriate.

If your child chooses not to comply with time-out displaying behavior that is more than mildly obstinate, it is appropriate to hold your child accountable for this behavior instead of just restricting privileges until your child complies with their time-out. A child may choose to hit, throw a tantrum, start to tear things up or display other intense reactions while not complying with their time-out. If so, use this Resource Guide to include in your Plan how you will effectively address these reactions. This may fit into your worse case scenario or other reactions you must Plan for.

Time-out in Your Child's Room

I love a time-out in the child's own room, on his own bed. When your child needs time away, time restricted from privileges, or you just need time to gather yourself, a time-out on a child's bed can be golden. Just for the sake of clarity, we are talking about kids past the toddler stage and definitely in their own bed. We'd never want to leave an infant or any child in a bed not his own or even in his own bed if he could be harmed by getting entangled, by suffocating and/or by any other means. We also want to make sure a child is old enough to fully understand the whole process, including why they are in time-out, and to learn from our training them to do a time-out as we expect.

A time-out on a child's own bed gives true time away and gives you time away also. When I require a time-out on the bed with my own kids, they have to stay on the beds with nothing else in the bed, except maybe the bedding and sometimes a book, until the time is up. Time-out on the bed allows the child to bear the weight of responsibility for her poor choices. If the child screams, cries, whines, etc., close the door and ignore. Put on some headphones as long as there's no danger that truly needs addressing. Go on with your life, and let your family go on with theirs.

When our children make poor choices, they often want others to suffer with them. Misery loves company. Time-out on his bed, in his room, by himself allows the child who made the bad choice to be the only one who is miserable. Even if you are bothered by your child's crying, whining, etc., pretend it doesn't bother you. Simply communicate to your child that you will not come in to talk with him until after he has clearly calmed down. It may take your child quite a while to calm down. That's okay. Worst-case scenario, he will fall asleep.

You will set the parameter that you, not your child, is in charge of when the time-out is over. This can be a set length of time, or it can have a condition such as, "I'll come talk with you when you are completely calm and ready to cooperate." An important rule is that you will have a calm, brief talk with your child before the time-out is over every time. This rule is extremely effective for several reasons. First, you get to briefly make sure your child understands why he was in time-out. Second, this communicates to your child that you are the boss. Third, your child will need to control himself either by staying on the bed for the allotted time, having to calm himself down or both. Fourth, this challenges your child to discipline himself to do what he ought to do instead of wandering out of his room to ask you if the time is up.

If you do decide to implement a condition such as, "I'll come talk with you when you are completely calm," make sure your child does not try to control or game you by calming down to get you to come in without being truly ready to listen and comply. If your child is giving you any backtalk, interrupting, continuing to act defiant, ramping right back up or acting like she doesn't want to listen during your brief conversation, do not accept any of this at all. It's a clear sign that your child is in battle or game mode, not cooperate mode. The Purpose is for your child to surrender her will, respecting your authority. You will see this when you remain firm and resolute with the time-out until your child is eager to comply. Hold out. Stick to your guns. Do not give in until your child surrenders. Surrender is your child lovingly, in action, saying, "I'm ready to listen, to cooperate, to trust you." This is your child channeling her energy into peace, cooperation, trust and love. This is exactly what you need to see. Accept nothing less.

In parenting, God sometimes gives us jewels we didn't expect. I initially had no idea how valuable it would be for my children to have a time-out on their beds. Sometimes I don't know what to do after my child makes a bad choice. I might be furious, confused or both. I have sent my child to his room with the command, "Get on your bed, and don't get up except to go to the bathroom and go right back." We spent the time on the front end training them not to get up or have anything in their beds and to be quiet. We had to be on top of the training process at first to deliberately help our children learn what was expected during a time-out. More monitoring was required at first, discipline included spankings if they did not comply, and perseverance was necessary to insist our children learned to meet our expectations when it came to a time-out. The time and effort to train our children to participate in a time-out as we expect is well worth it.

When you send your child to her room to have a time-out on her own bed, you will have time to calm down, think, discuss and pray about an appropriate response to whatever occurred. Our children don't need to know we are sometimes confused about what's right to do when dealing with them. Even if you need quite a while to think, pray and figure out the best next step, your child can just go to sleep if needed. No harm in that. What's important is that we don't forget or neglect the child and her needs while also not rushing ourselves either. It's important because we need to be fair and take the necessary time to reorganize. We make these choices in love to the best of our ability, not as a reaction to challenging feelings.

Sometimes, the time away will be the best punishment and also an intervention at the same time. After you feel an appropriate amount of time has passed, you may realize that the amount of time the child spent correctly participating in the time-out, even if he fell asleep part of the time, was adequate consequence. Base your decision on Godly wisdom, not feeling sorry for your child. Also, when you first send your child to his bed, don't feel pressured to set a time limit immediately. You can determine an appropriate length for the time-out and then communicate it to your child later, even if it's longer than the time he's spent already.

Time-out in the child's room, on the bed, can be a very effective discipline measure. For example, a lovingly firm consequence might be a child spending half a day or even all day in her room, on her bed, with nothing to do. This will not hurt your child when you factor in age and other important elements. Even a whole weekend can be done this way, but be careful with extended times like these. Consider your child's age and what the amount of time away might feel like to the child. The younger the child, the more the increments of time will be felt by them. For example, an hour might feel to a five-year-old like half a day to a ten-year-old. Also, make sure your child has an effective method of getting up to go to the bathroom and coming back as needed, a method you've wisely implemented to reduce the risk of them taking advantage of the situation.

Natural times to be with the family such as meal times can be a good break. It gives the child a break from the discipline in what needs to be a brief, positive time to connect with the family. The child gets a taste of what she is missing out on, everyone going about their lives in an enjoyable way. Don't fake this. Make sure you are working to create this in your home. Also, if a child is to have extended time in her room—like half a day, a full day, or for older children even a day and a half—as a part of strong, lovingly firm consequences, allow the child to have books to read.

Obviously, this wouldn't be a good choice if your child loves being alone and reading to the point that this would be like a reward to them; but it does give most children something to do for extended time-outs on their bed without undermining the effect of the discipline.

You get to decide as a part of your Plan what types of time-outs, if any, you believe will be Most Effective for your child. Use wisdom, regardless of what you choose. I cannot think of all the nuances for which you might need to account, including special health conditions; but this is where your expertise with your own child takes over. Use the elements you already have in place that you believe are effective, then tweak the rest into the Most Effective recipe for time-out options. From your new beginning of implementing your Plan, focus first on training your child to complete a time-out exactly as you expect. Whatever time you put in to train your child will reward you tremendously when it's time for a time-out.

EMOTIONS VS. BEHAVIOR: "MAD BUT NOT MEAN"

n love and healthy sensitivity to our children, we teach the distinction between their feelings and behavior. Most children 12 and under equate a feeling to a behavior. They will refer to "being mad" as yelling, stomping, hitting, not listening and so on. I explain this to kids in this way:

Me: "Mad is a feeling we have inside. It's not wrong to **feel** mad. (Place the emphasis on the fact that mad is a feeling.) When we get mad, we have angry thoughts like hitting, kicking, or not listening. Angry thoughts are normal and a part of feeling mad. It's not wrong to have an angry thought; we just have them."

I talk about this just a little and then ask the child a few questions:

Me: "Is it wrong to feel mad or angry?"
Child: "No."
Me: "And if I have angry thoughts, is it wrong to have angry thoughts?"
Child: "No."

I call this type of discussion "mad but not mean" or "mad but not bad," and it is a practical version of Ephesians 4:26a (KJV), *"Be ye angry, and sin not."* Most children will begin to grasp that angry feelings and angry thoughts are not wrong pretty quickly after this information is introduced.

Me: "Mad/anger is a feeling we have inside. We know it's not wrong to feel mad. And if I have angry thoughts, like hitting my brother, we know it's not wrong to just **think** (emphasis on *think,* highlighting that it's just a thought) about hitting him because angry thoughts are normal; but is it okay if you go ahead and **hit** (emphasis on *the behavior*) your brother?

Child: "No."

Me: "Why not?"

Child: "Because it's not wrong to be mad, but it's not okay to hit somebody. If I hit somebody, I'll get in trouble."

To hear a child 12 and under primarily equating the wrongdoing to getting in trouble is extremely age-appropriate. Children 12 and under, even though often bright intellectually, are developmentally concrete, black-and-white thinkers who relate to their world primarily through choices and consequences.

The "mad but not mean" concept is vital in caregiving in light of environmental and life changes that can cause your child to be hurt, scared, sad and mad. Nurture your child's feelings. Accept them and make it safe for your child to express his feelings through appropriate ways such as talking them out, taking a self-time-out, drawing, talking with a counselor, writing, and other ways you find are helpful to your child. It's important, though, to help your child understand through the "mad but not mean" concept that because you may have difficult feelings and thoughts, practicing self-control in the midst is essential and expected. This includes tantrums.

Because your 12-and-under child has gone through hurt, pain, break-ups, losses and challenges in life, must their continued response be aggression, destruction, shutting down or tantrums? If a child uses these maladaptive ways at first to communicate that they are going through something or that they need help, this is normal. If they display significant changes in behavior early on due to a trauma or problem, that also could be a sign of something significant bothering them. After they have been provided stability and help to effectively address the life challenge, we support their own healthy process through the "mad but not mean" concept.

Have absolute acceptance for your child's feelings and thoughts along with resolute Affirming Accountability for unhealthy choices. Even when there has been trauma and other difficult situations, at the right time of healing, helping your child distinguish feelings from actions and being held accountable accordingly empowers your child to push her energy into dealing with her problems in adaptive and healthy ways. Children absolutely need this. Maladaptive behavior can be a sign of struggle, yet children 12 and under benefit emotionally, behaviorally, personally and relationally from being challenged to work through their problems only in healthy ways. Self-control is the foundation of the healthy way. It's important that we embrace this as most kids don't need special accommodations when upset. What benefits kids 12 and under the most is being empowered to control themselves regardless of their emotions.

TRAINING YOUR CHILD TO ACCEPT LOVINGLY FIRM DISCIPLINE

Many caregivers immediately wonder how to deal with their child who will have major problems when they implement their Plan in earnest. How will your child react when you hold her accountable to your Expectation of Excellence? Will she become defiant? Will she have a meltdown? Will she become violent and/or destructive? Will she take out her anger on another person or threaten to harm herself? Reactions can range from difficult to dangerous.

I've met with caregivers who are terrified of how their kids will react to the diligence of Affirming Accountability. Caregivers have shared with me that they are afraid their child will throw huge fits, hurt other kids, tear up the house, try to attack them, become stubborn beyond belief, try to hurt himself, shut down, run away, not love them anymore and just give up on education, life and the future. What are the risks you face when you are resolute with Affirming Accountability? On the other hand, what are the risks your family and your child face if you continue on the path you are on without change? There are risks either way. You must decide which risk you are willing to take.

I truly have not seen many families that have created a loving Plan based on the L.E.A.P. process and implemented it consistently where their child has not gotten on board and overcome his problems in time. Children have God-given free will, though; and just like the story of the prodigal son in Luke 15, a child can choose to go the wrong way despite being raised in a loving environment. You cannot control this. What you can control is yourself and your environment. Use these in faith to do everything possible to challenge your child to grow strong in the Lord and within himself by preparing and executing your Plan.

In training your child to accept your lovingly firm discipline, we will focus on children primarily between the ages of four to twelve. Some caregivers might have three-year-olds whose intellect makes it suitable to include them in this discussion. Later in this section, we will focus specifically on toddlers from one to three years of age in their own labeled section. If you are working with a toddler, please read this entire section with the realization that not all of the principles will be suitable for their development yet. In the midst of working your Plan, some and maybe many of you will have to train your child to accept your lovingly firm discipline. Children know they need discipline; however, their primal instincts make them do whatever they can to avoid it. God has entrusted the child in your care to you. Use this information to help your child learn to succeed through L.E.A.P. and also to accept discipline instead of fighting against you when you implement it.

Our children's actions dictate our response. The tougher your child's reactions, the firmer your response must be. This is not an eye for an eye. This is meeting the challenge head on and standing firm. Let's discuss the essential steps for standing firm:

1. Face and accept your worst-case scenario.
2. Hold your child responsible.
3. Use powerful supports like police, hospital, family and mentor backup.
4. Get physical.
5. Go the extra mile.

Face and Accept Your Worst-Case Scenario

As we discussed in the section "Worst-Case Scenario," prevent what you can. Pretend the only one who is suffering and who will have to answer is your child; and do your best to make it so. Persevere until your child surrenders to you. Most of the time, children do not grow out of the problems they are having. The problems only become worse. Challenging your child's problem head on is a huge risk. The short-term risks are the reactions you fear your child will choose. The long-term risks involve your child spiraling slowly towards all the fears you have for his life. Face and accept your short-term worst-case scenario.

You know what your child might do. Prepare for it. This does not mean tiptoeing around the problem. If a bad storm is coming, we prepare. We plan ahead, get supplies, empty the grocery stores of all the milk and bread. We make sure there is enough room in the closet or the best place without windows. We gather candles. Also, we remain calm so our kids won't panic. What is your storm to come going to be like? What supplies do you need to prepare? How will you remain calm and weather the storm? If helpful, refer to Mark 4:35-41, a story about Jesus' presence and power in the midst of any storm.

Hold Your Child Responsible

Once a responsibility for your child is on the table, it stays on the table. Your child is responsible for removing the obstacle standing in the way of what's important for him. This may include disaster clean up. If your child wants to play Hurricane Ivan, well he had better prepare to be F.E.M.A. too. Hold your child accountable to his actions in a fair and appropriate way. This may include:

1. All privileges are on hold until your child takes your original command off of the table.
2. All privileges are on hold until your child cleans up the mess he made and/or repairs damages.

3. Extra work may be required equitable to the damage caused by the child.

4. Requiring the child to complete an amount of your home responsibilities equitable to the time you had to spend addressing/repairing the problems the child caused.

5. Enforcing firm and appropriate consequences equitable for the choices the child made amidst the storm the child caused.

We cannot prevent storms as they are out of our control. We can prepare for storms, protect who and what we can, and prohibit panic. In the aftermath, make sure the storm maker has the opportunity to be responsible for as much of the devastation as possible. Again, this is not retaliation, this is recompense. Recompense is experiential responsibility.

Use Powerful Supports

God gave your child to you. He has trusted you with your child. You can handle whatever your child needs you to handle.

> *No temptation has overtaken you except what is common to mankind. And God is faithful; he will not let you be tempted beyond what you can bear. But when you are tempted, he will also provide a way out so that you can endure it.*
> —1 Corinthians 10:13

You may be tempted to doubt yourself, God or your child. You surely may be ready to doubt me. That's okay. I accept that, but don't. Instead, gather powerful supports. These powerful supports may be the police, the hospital, family members and/or mentors. Use these as needed for safety, not because you are intimidated or defeated. If your child is threatening harm of others to a level you believe imminent, call the police. Do this because this is the right support. Remain calm and steadfast.

If your child threatens harm to himself, take him to a hospital for evaluation. When needed, invite a family member or mentor in to back you up, not take over. Be sure you are the one primarily addressing the situation. Do not act like you can't handle the situation. Show wisdom in getting support. Counseling can also be a powerful support. I've seen many caregivers who are doing an excellent job of raising their children choose counseling as a wise support. Do not choose any of these methods to threaten, intimidate or try to destroy your child's resolve. Do not bluff. Make a Plan which supports what you believe will be Most Effective in trying to deter harm and encourage civility on the part of your child, instead of trying to control them into behaving the way they should behave. Choose supports wisely. Implement supports courageously.

Get Physical

Most of discipline will involve exercising your mind, your authority, and your loving firmness with your child. However, there may be occasions where the best course of action will be to get physical.

Retaliation—like lashing out in frustration, using snide remarks, calling children names like lazy, ungrateful, etc., hitting (other than controlled, appropriate physical discipline), pushing, kicking, slapping or "popping" a child in the face or mouth, cursing at children or possibly around them—is harmful and can be damaging. From time to time, caregivers make these mistakes, which is not okay. If we have done any of these, we must do everything we can to correct and never repeat these mistakes. We must also not succumb to guilt that incapacitates us from figuring out how to be assertive with our children instead of aggressive.

When working with your child, it may be beneficial to use physical interventions at times. This is why your Plan is so important. Physical interventions should be neither reactionary nor based on feelings. Physical interventions must be action-based in line with what you believe is best to train your child and/or bring safety. Possible times for physical intervention include:

1. when you must stop a child from harming himself or others
2. when you need to enforce a boundary
3. when lovingly firm actions of authority are necessary

Children threaten harm in many ways. Be wise when it comes to this. Despite what your child has shown you, children can control themselves even when enraged. I have often seen enraged children who seem to be out of control, but they are in reality making deliberate choices. They choose to attack certain people in the family but not others, to break certain objects but not others, to break objects but not hit people, to scream, cry and threaten but not follow through. One child hit herself in the head during episodes of intense conflict with her mom as a way of hurting her mom emotionally because she didn't want the problems associated with attacking her mom physically. Even though your child doesn't display control, this doesn't mean that your child cannot employ control.

Be wise when your child threatens harm or acts in a dangerous way. Not all children will truly hurt themselves or others. I've seen a great number of children bang their heads or punch something without causing any significant hurt or damage in actuality. None of us caregivers want to see our children make these choices. The key to being the Most Effective is discerning what is going on with your child. Is your child going far enough to truly harm herself or someone else? Do you need to physically intervene or not?

When in doubt, err on the side of caution. At the same time, your discernment will help you respond appropriately. You don't want to under respond when there is true danger; however, you don't want to overreact when your child is trying to manipulate the situation or carrying through with threats that have no true substance behind them.

When you feel you must physically intervene, do so with the least amount of physical intervention necessary. If your child is banging her head, you may be able to slide something soft that won't cause suffocation or a hand in between. If your child is trying to hurt another person, you may need to physically block the way. In some cases, you may need to restrain your child. Be very cautious if you feel your child might possibly be too big to handle without endangering either of you or causing the situation to evolve into a WWE event.

When physical intervention is necessary and you can calmly intervene, do so in a manner to bring safety. In these situations, the tacit message is, "You are choosing not to control yourself and bringing danger, therefore I will intervene."

If you choose to engage physically with a therapeutic hold you have sufficient knowledge to implement, one that you are confident brings safety and not further danger, you must outlast your child. Hold your child in a way that doesn't hurt them or put any type of unhealthy physical pressure on them until they surrender, not just pause. Say once every minute or so, "When you are calm and quiet, I will let you go." Physical restraints from a parent must always be wise and well prepared in advance.

Physical Intervention to Enforce Boundaries

An example of "getting physical" in a healthy way involves Bill's mom. Bill, around the age of four, was aggressive to his mom. She and he were of a size that she could physically intervene safely and effectively when he tried to be aggressive with her. She would prevent aggression by being mindful that it could happen at any time and positioning her body so she could intercept him if necessary. She remained calm or pretended she was calm even when aggressive episodes occurred and she felt afraid, angry or extremely frustrated. When Bill tried to attack her, she would extend her arms and keep him at arms' length so he couldn't get to her. As she implemented her Plan, she also found a way to hold firmly onto his wrists to restrain him effectively without hurting him. Bill's mom always Persevered until Bill completely stopped his aggressive episode and was willing to comply.

Physical intervention can be used effectively to enforce a boundary. What Bill's mom did was a form of enforcing a boundary, her body, from Bill's attacks. Some other examples of boundaries might be your child staying in his room, on his bed, or staying away from other people or items he is trying to hurt or damage in some way. If you choose to physically intervene to enforce a boundary, Plan well and be very deliberate. Here are keys:

1. Compose yourself and intervene firmly, yet not forcefully.

2. If the need arises to physically intervene to prevent harm or enforce a boundary, be wise. Make sure you feel confident in your ability to intervene safely and effectively. If your child physically struggles against you to the point that you might not be able to manage the struggle safely, stop. We'll review an example of a situation in which you would stop later on.

3. Use very few words, if any. If you do need to speak, use a firm "No!" If needed, state once every minute or so something like, "Go to your room and calm down," or "The longer you disobey, the more consequences there are going to be." You can also make a statement like the following before you walk away: "Come find me when you are ready to listen." The latter is a part of avoiding unhealthy power struggles. Just make sure your child doesn't participate in privileges and does not represent danger to himself anyone else while not in your presence.

Let's discuss what to do when a child physically struggles against you to the point that you might not be able to manage the struggle safely. I'll use the example of six-year-old Victor who was walked to his room for a time-out on his bed. He not only refused to stay on his bed but wanted to leave his room. His mother stood in the doorway, confident that she was physically able to enforce the boundary of him not leaving his room without much of a power struggle. Unexpectedly, Victor was stronger and more determined than she thought and pushed at her bullishly to get out of his room. No matter how self-controlled his mother remained, Victor's forcefulness caused his mom to expect that one or both of them could get hurt. She decided to change her tactics and moved from the doorway.

Victor ran out of his room and around the house. His mom did not chase him, but she felt flustered and confused. After a moment, she refuted the lie that she was failing and composed herself. She kept her wits about her. Victor grabbed a snack he was not supposed to have and began watching TV. His mom didn't know what to do. She felt almost powerless, and definitely like her son was winning. She reminded herself, "I'm not powerless. I can do this."

She kept an eye on Victor as he watched TV while pondering, "What can I do?" Taking a breath, she prayed and re-centered herself on the L.E.A.P. process she had in place with her son. She decided, "I will remember my process and stick to my Plan."

If you ever get into a situation where you try to intervene according to the comprehensive Plan you have developed and it doesn't work, bring yourself back your L.E.A.P. process and your Plan. Situations may shake you. L.E.A.P. and your Plan will be your foundation in this effort. Victor's mom collected herself. She reminded herself that she had an already developed L.E.A.P process and she used it guide her. Here's how she thought through the situation:

L – What are the most Loving and firm ways I can act in this situation?

- Remain calm.
- Be strong and firm instead of angry or emotional in my attitude.

E – What is my Expectation of Excellence for my child?

- My Expectation of Excellence for my son is, "You will do what you are told the first time."

A – What options do I have for Affirming Accountability after what Victor has done? I can...

- Turn off the TV.
- Take the snack and remote from Victor.
- Tell Victor commandingly, "Go to your room!" (Give this command up to three times in a loud and commanding voice without

yelling.) If he doesn't go to his room after the third command, tell him that he will get a spanking if he doesn't go right away.

- Spank Victor firmly and effectively if he does not go to his room right then.
- Give Victor extended time in his room since he chose to run out of the room instead of obeying originally.

Other variations include:

- Using firm authority, take Victor by the arm and lead him to his room.
- Tell Victor, "Go to your room" in a serious, quiet, commanding voice. (Sometimes a serious almost whisper can be an effective alternative).
- If you choose not to spank, choose alternative "next level" appropriate discipline that you believe will firmly reinforce the importance of complying from the beginning. Ex. Not being able to participate in a significant fun event.

P – How do I Persevere?

- Victor never completed the original punishment of a time-out on his bed before he ran out of his room. Victor must still complete this time-out and any additional consequences for his further disobedience before his privileges are restored.
- Safely stop him if he tries to hit me, and call his uncle or the police only if necessary.
- Project strength.
- Outlast him until he chooses to surrender to my loving authority.

Sometimes your child will battle you while you are holding him Accountable. Your feelings may prompt you to want to give up. Don't. Take a step back and pray. When you feel like you don't know what to do, follow the PRP steps (pray, refocus, pretend):

1. Pray for strength and wisdom.

When you are feeling defeated, pray. You will ultimately succeed because you have what no human can offer, wisdom from God. Ask God for wisdom in faith, and He will give it to you.

> *If any of you lacks wisdom, you should ask God, who gives*
> *generously to all without finding fault, and it will be given*
> *to you. But when you ask, you must believe and not doubt,*
> *because the one who doubts is like a wave of the sea, blown*
> *and tossed by the wind. That person should not expect to*
> *receive anything from the Lord.*
>
> —James 1: 5-7

2. Refocus on your L.E.A.P process.

You've worked hard to develop your L.E.A.P. process and your Plan. It's time to evaluate the step of Affirming Accountability. Ask yourself, according to what my child has done, what do I think will be the best ways to hold him Accountable? How do I make the "punishment" fit the "crime"? Write down your thoughts if you need to.

3. Pretend you know exactly what you are doing.

Fake it 'til you make it. Stay calm and resolved. Act like you know what you are doing as a loving authority. This is important because your child doesn't know when you don't know. Use the wisdom God gave you to the best of your ability in that specific situation. Persevere until your child surrenders to your loving authority by accepting the specified consequences. After the situation, evaluate your actions in prayer, to gain more wisdom as you help your child transform. You can do this.

Physical Intervention with Toddlers

Physically intervening with your child may be beneficial to enforce your lovingly firm authority. This section is primarily directed toward children under the age of four. We must proceed with great Purpose and understanding to protect a child's spirit, mind and heart while training a toddler to respect loving authority.

It is natural and developmentally appropriate for young children to explore their world. However, toddlers do not understand the world, their environment or dangers as we do. Therefore, it's important to be deliberate with boundaries early on, using the word "no" reinforced by physically enforcing your lovingly firm authority. If a toddler starts to touch something she shouldn't touch, say "no" firmly. Repeat a second time if necessary. If the toddler doesn't obey after the second command, act. Here are the keys:

1. Remove the object.
2. Remove your toddler from being in a position to interact with the object.
3. Place yourself as a barrier between your toddler and the object if necessary.

Our physical intervention enforces our lovingly firm authority in a deliberate but non-aggressive way. Be deliberate, not aggressive. Try to not huff, puff, snatch, or verbally or physically express frustration. Act in line with the three keys of removing the object, removing your toddler or using a safe physical barrier, including yourself. Show your toddler that you mean what you say by enforcing your "no." It is normal that you might have to do this several times. Be creative, but do not bribe a toddler. Let your no be no.

I know telling a child "no" is not popular with some; however, your child learning to obey your "no" might save her life. What if she is about to grab something dangerous? Training your child to respect your "no" can help her stop in her tracks instead of getting hurt. We can't be within arms' reach every second.

If a toddler continues to try to touch an object after twice being told "no," it can be appropriate to give the child two or three smacks on the hand or the bottom; however, be very judicious with this response. If a toddler reaches for an object after being told "no" twice, while this can seem like defiance, it may not be. It's best to think first of physically removing either the object or the child or physically blocking the child from the object. It may be appropriate to distract your child with another object as long as it's not a bribe with a treat.

If it definitely seems like defiance or some other inappropriate behavior, then two or three smacks on the hand or bottom may be appropriate. One to three spanks on the buttocks with your hand must be hard enough to communicate you mean business but absolutely not bruise. This can be appropriate physical discipline for a child over 14 months and under the age of 4. Your child must be of an age and level of intelligence that you are confident your child understands why he received swats or spanks. Use Godly wisdom. Act with intention. Avoid reacting out of frustration.

Physical intervention to enforce your lovingly firm authority can also mean having your child go to a certain place, especially for toddlers. If so, take your toddler firmly by the hand, arm or shoulder. Escort, never drag. If the child chooses not to go willingly, you might pick up your toddler and carry her where you want her to go. Avoid acting in frustration. This will cause your child to sense that you can't handle her. Be intentional, firm, serious, and controlled both emotionally and physically.

For children, between the ages of one and three, physically enforcing a boundary such as not getting up from a time-out must be implemented wisely, boldly and safely. Some of you may need to put a very young child back in time-out over and over. This is to communicate with your actions, "This is what I expect, and this will happen." Communicate confidence, not frustration. If you choose the method of putting your child back in time-out over and over until he stays there, do so without much emotion. Your child may want to make it a game and will be more enticed to do so if you act exasperated or indicate through words or behavior that your child is getting the best of you.

Be intentional until your child recognizes he cannot get over on you and decides to push his energy into controlling himself instead of against you. Remember to use a reasonable amount of time to start with when training your child to do time-out as you expect such as 30 seconds to a minute.

As you consistently hold your child Accountable to stay in time-out as you expect, move both the amount of time up to an appropriate level incrementally and physically from standing close to your child to further away as your child is learning to comply.

Physically block your child's path to enforce her staying in her room if appropriate as long as the situation makes sense, especially with a smaller child. Do not go "toe to toe" with any child. You cannot control your child. You can control yourself and your environment. Shut down all privileges until your child takes obeying you off the table through her actions. If this means you have to refuse access to every electronic device in your house to enforce the restriction of privileges until your child honors the original boundary, then so be it. Prevent yourself from being undermined. Prepare the rest of the family to enjoy regular life as much as possible. Pretend you are as content as ever. Persevere until your child surrenders to your loving authority. Make sure you are never applying physical pressure on your child out of frustration, regardless of your child's age. This is not only wrong, but also completely ineffective; doing this tells your child you can't handle him. Be purposeful in everything you do with Affirming Accountability when you choose to physically intervene and Persevere. Pray for strength and wisdom, and God will give it to you.

It's Okay to Be Angry When You Physically Intervene with Your 12 and Under

When I was a young child, I hated needles. In fact, I still hate needles, but the context is when I was a young child. My mom would take me to a clinic periodically to get my wellness shots. Every time we pulled into the parking lot and I saw the ominous blue building, I went crazy. My mom would literally have to drag me kicking and screaming the whole way. I never thought about this, but as hysterical as I was, I remember now that my mom wasn't. She didn't yell, scream, curse or show her frustration or embarrassment through her actions toward me. She pushed, pulled and carried my body with determination, not displaced aggression, to get me in the clinic. She had my older sister along to help as a powerful support.

If you are going to physically intervene with your child in any way, it's okay to feel angry, frustrated and exasperated. The Bible says in Ephesians 4:26, "Be angry." That's so cool and understanding of God. Then God finishes that sentence with "...and sin not." So, we are apparently able to be angry without sinning.

Focus your anger on the problem your child is struggling with and the enemy's attempts to hurt us, not on your child. Accepting our feelings is healthy for us and can teach your child to accept his own feelings, whatever they may be. Controlling ourselves regardless of how we feel must be an example we set as well.

> *For God has not given us a spirit of fear and timidity, but of power, love, and self-discipline.*
> —2 Timothy 1:7

We must always act in line with a spirit of self-discipline. Appropriate spankings in the context of the loving relationship truly do not teach children to hit and be aggressive. Lashing out in reaction to anger or frustration causes children to learn to do the same. My mom physically intervened with me because she knew the shots would help me. She was never aggressive in the process. Even when my mom spanked, she was intentional about discipline; it was not an outpouring of her own pain on me. Be determined, without aggression, if you choose to physically intervene.

Physical Intervention to Enforce Your Lovingly Firm Authority

Firm physical interventions, even spankings, administered appropriately on the foundation of a loving bond will not leave bruises on your child's heart or body. Be resolute. Be firm. Be unwavering in holding your child Accountable. Show your child what it means to be angry and sin not. Show your child the truth, which is that physical discipline, even spanking, does not teach a child to be aggressive. Unleashing our own anger on or around children, either verbally or physically, is what teaches them to unleash their anger. When you are angry yet controlled in your physical interventions, you will teach your child in powerful and effective ways to change.

Your child will clearly understand firm and appropriate physical intervention/discipline in the context of a loving relationship. This may include spankings. Healthy, effective physical discipline must take into account many factors including age, intellect, relational appropriateness, the law, and your process, to name just a few. I will discuss spankings later, how kids value them, and how to make them appropriate and effective. For now, let's embrace that the loving relationship is strong enough to hold every ounce of healthy discipline necessary to help your child succeed.

We don't have to be physically strong to win the battle against the influences trying to stand in the way of our child's potential. Let's work to ensure that our bond with our child is strong…that our commitment to self-control is strong. Let's be strong in seeking the Lord's wisdom and not trying to be wise in our own eyes. Let's be strong enough to push aside our pride and accept help. If your child becomes absolutely unruly, do not try to force your child to do anything. Try instead to be a force that compels your child to do everything. Hold your Expectation in priority to everything else, save what is necessary. Intervene physically when it makes sense in order to train your child, but avoid it at all costs when complete control and fairness are not attached.

SURRENDER

read that Milton Erickson, a famous family psychiatrist and psychologist, tells a story involving one of his daughters when she was very young. The story goes something like this...Erickson's young daughter disrespected her mom one night. Erickson told her to go apologize. "I don't has to," his daughter replied. Erickson took hold of her leg just firmly enough so she couldn't run away from him. She said, "Let go!" He replied, "I don't have to." His daughter cried and pleaded with him to let go. He held on. Because she was unable to get out of the hold, she agreed she would tell her mom she was sorry. He held on. She expressed that she needed to go tell her mom she was sorry. He didn't let go. After a long while, his daughter expressed, "I'm really sorry; I want to go tell mommy sorry." He let her go.

I'm so thankful for the children God gave me through marriage and biologically. My sons through marriage were older when Jen and I got together, and they grew strong. They loved tests of strength such as arm wrestling. One particular test of strength came against my teenage son through marriage in his lean, football-playing shape vs. my middle age, not-so-football-playing shape. He was stronger than me physically, but I knew I needed to win. We grabbed onto a bar above our heads, lifted our feet at the same time and hung there holding our weight. I knew one thing, one win would go a long way. I pretended I didn't hurt while he grunted. I pretended I could hang there all day all the while praying to God that he would let go. I hid my strain and remained resolved to win. I did win in the end, in large part because I chose to be stronger mentally and through praying while outwardly convincing my son that he couldn't beat me.

When you and your child become locked in a battle, for the sake of your child, you must win. You will not win through lashing out in anger. You will win by remaining steadfast, calm, sure of your Purpose and victory. Your victory is not over your child. Your victory will be over the pernicious destruction coming out in your child's choices. The enemy wants us to think the fight is between you and your child, but it's not—though it is a battle all the same. Regardless of how you feel on the inside, project confidence on the outside and win each battle that corresponds with your one specific Expectation of Excellence.

Surrender during a battle is when both of you are exhausted, but your child is the one who gives in. Your child will have a clear attitude of, "Okay. I'm done fighting you. I give up. I want to do good. What do you want me to do?" When that attitude is genuine, it will not be accompanied by any sassiness nor will it ramp back up into another fight right away. When you hold out for surrender, you will be able to physically see it when your child reaches that point. Each time your child surrenders, your child will fully let go of the immediate gratification she was caught up in and decide to fully trust you with every fiber of her being.

Hold out firmly for your Expectation until your child surrenders. When that happens, your child will master himself in that moment and surrender his will to yours. The surrendering of will to a loving authority bent on acting in their best interest is the exact relationship children are meant to have with their caregivers. We are children of God. Submitting to God does not crush the spirit. Surrender to a loving authority liberates the spirit. When your child experiences surrender of will, and thus that liberation of his spirit, he will comply and feel better. This is when he realizes that he caused all his own wasted time and suffering during his non-beneficial processes. Children also will experience that winning against their impulses, instead of winning against their caregivers, feels better to them relationally and to their conscience, as well as fostering belief in their own abilities. After the surrender occurs, don't hesitate to still impose some restrictions in response to your child's choices during the fight against you, when appropriate.

Your child must believe he can't beat you in order to eventually stop trying. Your child will then battle against his impulses instead of you. That is when your child will gain true victory evidenced by steps towards mastery over himself. Winning each battle, specifically in line with your Expectation of Excellence, is the Most Effective way to help your child redirect his energy positively.

During the battles, your child may take a break. It might seem that she is giving up the unhealthy behavior. Be careful. Do not accept half-hearted efforts. At times, you might be tempted to accept little signs of improvement as surrender just so the battle will be over. You'll want to accept that small drink of improvement after being in the desert of full-scale war for so long. Don't. Persevere, and not until your child just pauses or throws out some little improvement to try to get by. Hold on like Erickson did until your child fully surrenders during that battle to your loving authority and wants to meet your Expectation with nothing less than Excellence.

"GO THE EXTRA MILE"

The first step for many of you in going the extra mile is having complete faith that your child is capable of achieving your Expectation of Excellence. Doubt is present for many of you due to the ongoing battles and the repeated problems. Sometimes even medical professionals contribute to the idea that your child may not be able to control himself or change in the way you hope. Go the extra mile with faith that your child can change and your child is capable. Without the courage to fully pursue the principles in this book based on belief in God, your child and yourself, your efforts will lack conviction, consistency, and the power it takes to operate in the 97% to 98% range of the Most Effective Actions on a daily basis to help your child succeed. With faith, even if you just choose a full effort trial for six months, you will be successful in being as effective as you need to be to help your child succeed.

Everything you do will be intentional. Caregivers have removed everything from their child's room, shut off the internet, and called the police. Stand behind your hopes and your Purpose for your child. Do what it takes to reinforce that you will not waiver in holding him to an Expectation of Excellence. Do not settle for less. Go as far as you need to go in love; however, never cross a line of trying to make your child do something. You do not control your child. Your child has God-given free will. This is not about a "Well, I'll show you attitude." This is about communicating to your child:

I love you. We cannot get along and you cannot get along in this world while making those poor choices. I believe you are capable of stopping those choices. I am facing my fears of your failure and you choosing to go the wrong way. I will do what it takes to back up what I say. If I say no TV, I will physically remove the TV from the house if I have to in order to enforce this. My belief in you and my dedication to something better will not waiver. I will hold you accountable equal to my belief in you. I will not do anything to try to harm you because you hurt me. I will not unleash my anger on you. I will intentionally act to bring us closer to each other and support you in mastering yourself. I will control myself first and expect you to do the same. I will not waiver in my high expectation of my own self-control, and I will expect no less of you. We can do this, together!

Going the extra mile for some of you may include spanking. Caregivers fear spanking for many reasons; however, firm and appropriate spankings are always an extension of love. Other actions to beat, harm, intimidate and control children are called "spankings," but they are not the same. We will go into detail in the section on spankings.

Your child needs your boldness in love to hold her accountable. If your child 12 and under needs a spanking, then spank. If your child needs to see you stand for safety by calling the police, then call the police. If your child threatens to hurt herself and you need to take her to the hospital to be assessed each and every time she does, then take her to the hospital. If your child needs you to allow her to fail, allow her to fail. What your child doesn't need is for you to do for her what she can do for herself, protect them from the lovingly firm discipline of other caregivers they know love them, or overprotect/enable them to spare yourself pain or assuage guilt.

Disciplining your child firmly may be painful to you. Your child knows that you love him. You will not lose your relationship. Your child will not hate you. I've never heard an adult say, "I wish my caregivers had been too lenient on me." Focus on your Purpose beyond the pain. Remember the life skills that are essential to your child making it in this world. Remember the opportunity for better relationships. Remember your Purpose for your child; in moments of doubt, hold fast to your Purpose to allow you to not shrink back because of the pain, worry, fear, false guilt and doubt. Give God your worry, guilt, shame, embarrassment and fear. One of my favorite verses for overcoming anxiousness is Philippians 4: 4-7 (NIV):

> *Rejoice in the Lord always. I will say it again: Rejoice! Let your gentleness be evident to all. The Lord is near. Do not be anxious about anything, but in every situation, by prayer and petition, with thanksgiving, present your requests to God. And the peace of God, which transcends all understanding, will guard your hearts and your minds in Christ Jesus.*

Rejoice! The victory is already yours. Release your anxiousness. Begin thanking God right now for the victory and allow His peace to guard your heart and mind. Do this over and over and over while being very firm with your strong-willed child until your faith is rewarded with having your child back.

Prepare your Plan to account for any of the challenging reactions your child might display in response to the weight of responsibility. Allow your child to see that you want your child to have all of his privileges—but respect, responsibility and/or relationships take priority over everything non-essential. Train your child to accept discipline according to your Expectation. Intervene physically only in appropriate ways when necessary to protect, enforce a boundary or reinforce your Expectation. Make sure you have strategized how to do physical intervention with your child safely and effectively without it turning into a brawl. Go the extra mile wisely in line with your Purpose and belief. Be intentional, and choose actions that reinforce what you have said while avoiding unhealthy emotion and commotion. Be sure your child knows that you love her. Ask for wisdom from God and advice from wise people you can trust. Pray, fast, hope in the Lord. Persevere through that extra mile.

SPANKING

Affirmation, Correction, Affirmation

What is the purpose of spanking? To inflict a measured amount of pain for the child's benefit

When is spanking appropriate? When an adult is in control of himself; when the discipline fits the child's needs and the offense; when a child is over the age of 18 months at a minimum and mainly over the age of 2 up to 11 or 12 years of age

Why is spanking important? To help young children make an important connection in the brain between an unhealthy choice and a painful outcome to encourage them to direct their energy into a healthy choice

Where do I spank? In private, on the buttocks; also, one to three smacks on the hand may be appropriate for little children from one to three years of age

Who needs to spank? Only those whom the child being spanked knows loves them

Who needs to be spanked? Only children whose temperament, level of understanding and situation require it

How do I spank appropriately and effectively?

That's a great question. Let's explore this together. This section is admittedly one of the most difficult to cover—not because we don't know the truth about lovingly firm spankings, but because the enemy works so hard to destroy and pervert the truth about appropriate spankings. I trust God for His victory in this area, that we may embrace the truth about appropriate spankings and discern how to proceed in love.

Our children need us to know the truth about appropriate spankings. You may or may not decide to spank your child. That will be fine as long as you've made that choice based on what's best for your child. Unfortunately, popular opinion doesn't help much. Many people are finding experts who say we should not spank because it's harmful to children. On the other hand, many caregivers tell me they have people in their lives telling them that if they would just spank the child, the problems would all go away. What's the truth? What's best for your child?

Answering the first question, what's the truth, will give you the information you need to discern what's best for your child. Our truth comes from the real-life experiences of caregivers who have spanked only with control, in wisdom and on the foundation of a loving relationship (according to the child's view, not the adult's). Most importantly, the experiences of children who have been spanked appropriately advocate for the purpose of effective and appropriate spankings. In this case, we get to learn from the experts, the ones experiencing spankings and how those spankings truly affect them.

The awesome fact about appropriate spankings is that kids themselves advocate for them. It's interesting how our kids know what they need, even when it's unpleasant. So often in my office, I am shocked by how kids will state clearly what's most beneficial for them; and they often advocate for appropriate spankings…for themselves! When I first started advocating for caregivers to use lovingly firm discipline with their children, I expected the children to hate me or to be mad and angry; but they weren't! They aren't! When children get lovingly firm discipline, including appropriate spankings, in the context of a loving relationship, they not only accept that completely but express that the discipline, the spankings, help them! This is why I get so discouraged when I read another expert saying that appropriate spankings harm children. This is just not true. The fact is that we are doing pernicious harm to our children by not understanding and embracing the truth about appropriate spankings. We will face the truth courageously together, and I trust God to guide you from there.

Caregivers who come to my office cringe when they tell me they spank their children. They often reflexively lower their heads a bit and just about mumble, "I spank," expecting some type of reprimand. It's awesome when they lift their heads in relief to my response when I express that there is absolutely nothing wrong with appropriate spankings. That's the key, though; I support *appropriate* spankings.

Much controversy surrounds spankings. Let's get beyond the controversy. Let's talk about why we are doing all of this—for our kids. I'm writing this book to advocate for our kids, and you are reading this book to advocate for yours. In order for us to truly advocate for our children, we must embrace the truth about spanking.

First let's embrace that spanking is difficult. Inflicting pain on our children is painful for everyone involved. Of course some people have twisted their own whims and desires to their own selfishness in the name of "spanking." These people will always exist—and their actions will always be wrong. For those of you who had someone unleash their anger and beat you or mistreat you emotionally, verbally and/or physically because they decided to take their pain out on you or around you, the idea of spanking can be terrifying. When an adult lashes out at a child in the name of discipline, this is actually punishing a child for upsetting, disturbing, hurting, embarrassing or frustrating said adult. Sometimes adults punish children just for being there. Whatever the reason or the cause, an adult punishing/ unleashing anger on a child is never about the child.

An adult taking their pain out on a child in the name of discipline or around a child hurts a child on the inside. The pain the child internalizes crushes the spirit. Children that have anger, frustration, or pain unleashed on them and/or around them feel confused, afraid in an unhealthy way, and over time, bitter. "Discipline without relationship breeds rebellion," we've heard it said. I've taken this a step further: discipline without relationship breeds resentment, and resentment breeds rebellion.

Kids that are being abused typically don't rebel directly. They are too afraid of more abuse. These children most often build resentment, and the resentment comes out in passive-aggressive ways. The children develop a problem that can't be pinned on rebellion. I've heard teens share after overcoming relational challenges with their caregivers that they stopped trying to succeed in life as a passive-aggressive way to get back at their caregivers.

Let's first embrace that none of us are or ever should be abusers of our children. I've known caregivers to go too far when disciplining their children. I've made mistakes unintentionally while disciplining as well. My hope is that we understand that as caregivers we will make mistakes although we must try desperately not to. We never want to hurt our child's heart or crush her spirit. When we make mistakes as caregivers, they must be honest mistakes because we were trying to get it right but messed up. When it comes to discipline, we must be careful not to make mistakes and also to overcome our own fear so we are not hindered from acting in love according to our child's needs.

A speeding ticket today will be painful, but less painful than a car crash in the future. Appropriate and Effective spankings can be one of today's "speeding tickets." The truth is, when a child knows he is loved, a fair and appropriate spanking only hurts the body, not the heart or the spirit. Spankings also do not teach children to hit, as some claim. Aggression begets aggression. When a person lashes out at a child or around a child due to their own unfettered anger, this is harmful aggression. This is what teaches children to be aggressive when angry in return. To be angry and sin not, we remain angry yet in control.

I've almost always been angry when I've spanked my children. I am angry at the wrong they've done and the hurt they've caused. I'm angry that they didn't obey me. I'm angry because they made a choice detrimental to themselves and others. Despite our feelings of anger, which are normal as caregivers, we keep control of our actions. At times, we all will feel angry and frustrated with our children about their behavior. Don't take their choices or their comments personally. Choose what you believe is the most intentional and helpful way to respond. Sometimes that means allowing the pain of natural consequences. For example, a child choosing to disobey at dinner time by running around and not eating what you've prepared may mean that your child misses eating dinner due to your clearly defined expectation that they eat at the specified dinner time or else miss dinner. The hunger of choosing not to eat dinner at the specified time would be a natural consequence of the child's chosen actions.

Both natural consequences and imposed consequences can be painful. They must be painful to an effective degree, or they have the illusion of being beneficial when they are not in actuality. We as caregivers are not there to pile on the pain. We also must not try to save our children from every bit of pain. Just like an autoimmune system gets stronger from being exposed to various bacteria, our children get stronger by being allowed to learn from their mistakes.

Jesus did not save Judas or Peter from the consequences of their actions in the final days of His life. Judas betrayed Jesus and hung himself. Peter betrayed Jesus and came back stronger as one of His most ardent followers. We want to protect our children from unnecessary pain, but learning from our choices is necessary pain intended to give us the opportunity to learn valuable lessons and grow. The risk is that our children may choose to follow the ways of Judas rather than Peter. We cannot choose for them. We also need to avoid giving our children an artificial view of life by shielding them from the consequences of choices they make. To do so sets up our children for a slow and pernicious course of not being able to master themselves and the ensuing higher risk of failure in their lives. Our goal as caregivers is to equip and empower...not enable. I will say this, though: empowering our choice-and-consequence learners with Affirming Accountability on the foundation of the loving bond based on our belief in their ability provides one of the most powerful influences towards Peter's outcome that a child can have.

Children age 12 and under are mentally black-and-white, choice-and-consequence learners. Children of these ages most often equate good choices to being good themselves and bad choices to being bad themselves. Based on the biological development of children, not a biological deficiency, it is natural for children under the age of 12 to have significant challenge overcoming their desire to give in to their feelings and impulses in a given moment. When they do give in to their feelings and impulses, resulting in what they know is a bad choice, children often feel oppressed by the choice they made. It can seem like low self-esteem when children say, "I'm bad! Mommy, please help me! I want to be good but I can't!" Caregivers report their children making these statements with utter heartbreak. It may seem that children 12 and under who make these statements are suffering from poor self-esteem, but they are not. Children are revealing to us their truth: they want to do good, but they can't seem to do the good they want to do consistently. This is because they continually fall into the trap of choosing the path of least resistance, giving in to their feelings and impulses in the moment.

Children are designed by God to need our help in controlling themselves emotionally and behaviorally. The prefrontal cortex of the brain responsible for emotional regulation, impulse control and decision making is the final part of the brain to fully develop when a person is near their mid-twenties. Many children are focused on trying to control their world to suit what works best for them rather than trying to control their impulses and emotions. What we adults see is maladaptive behavior, but to our children, this behavior equals the most immediately gratifying path for them. The most gratifying path in the moment is often the most unhealthy path in the long run. In order to empower our children to direct their energy into healthier choices, God designed caregivers to be a pseudo-frontal lobe for our kids.

As adults, our developed executive functioning center, our prefrontal cortex, helps us evaluate life in healthy ways. We understand choices and consequences. We slow down when a police officer is on the road, people straighten up when the boss is around, we take out the garbage and pay our bills to avoid pain and problems. Your 12 and under child does not have a fully developed prefrontal cortex. Your child is developing morals and character but still has a long way to go. Your child also is likely motivated from within to have life on her terms. What your child has now as one of her greatest resources is you. Your child needs you to lovingly, consistently, and courageously guide her choices. She is struggling and failing because she does not have the internal motivation or strength to overcome her feelings and impulses without your direct, consistent intervention. Your Most Effective empowerment comes through meeting your 12 years and under child where she is, to help her learn from her choices through appropriate consequences.

Consequences just means the result of a decision. Right choices lead to many healthy consequences a child can enjoy such as avoiding getting into trouble, enjoying regular privileges, and feeling good about the choice he made when he reflects later. Right doing equals right feeling. Children feel happier and better when they are making right choices. Poor choices can lead to many healthy consequences from which a child can learn. When our child is continually struggling, he often needs the pain of natural and imposed consequences to help him redirect his energy into healthier patterns.

Our children need discipline. Discipline means to teach. I wish we as humans were not creatures that often need pain to motivate us, but a fact of our human nature is that we often do. When do we go to the dentist, stop speeding or often stop doing pleasurable but detrimental activities in our lives? Sometimes it's due to pain, which can be a powerful motivator. Now pain can be inflicted by those who neither know us nor care about us or pain can be allowed by those who love us. The same way that a battlefield surgeon might cut off a wounded leg that is infected, another surgeon, especially one that cared about the patient, might want to see if the leg could be saved. The second surgeon painstakingly commits to a long and painful process by which the patient has an opportunity to get better and keep the leg.

Reward charts, stern looks, lectures, time-outs and even light spankings that really don't hurt can work well with children operating with the compliant and slow-to-warm-up temperamental affinities. Given their internal desires to please and not make waves respectively, they have strong internal motivations to please the boss or not upset the boss. These internal motivations make milder forms of correction work; however, these methods are not effective on a lasting basis for children operating with the strong-willed temperamental affinity who do not want to please the boss; instead, they want to be the boss. Often, these children need more structure and more lovingly firm discipline.

Why do children operating with the strong-willed temperamental affinity need firmer discipline? They are not internally motivated to please, get along, seek approval and follow the rules. They are internally motivated to find the most effective way to get their way or get out of what they don't want. Children operating with the strong-willed temperamental affinity are neither bad nor evil; they are driven. They are internally driven to get what they do want and out of what they don't want, and they will find what they consider the most effective means to do so.

Our children, at appropriate times, for appropriate reasons, in appropriate relationships and in appropriate measure may need spankings—just not all children, not all the time, not if the relational bond is not there, and not too hard or too soft. "Just right" spankings as a part of the discipline package cause children to want to push their energy away from choices that led to the spanking and toward healthier decisions.

The loving relationship can contain every ounce of healthy and firm discipline necessary to help a child succeed. Appropriate spankings in the context of a loving relationship do not hurt a child's heart, nor in any way do they crush a child's spirit. I've spanked my kids very firmly, and our relationship was not hurt. I've seen countless caregivers spank their kids with no hurt to relationship or the kids' spirit whatsoever. Let's embrace the truth: healthy spankings, in the right context, can and will hurt your child's body, but they will not hurt your child's heart or spirit. In fact, very firm and appropriate spankings can help liberate your child's spirit.

Your child's spirit will be liberated because that specific pain, for specific reasons that your child knows are not good for them, will challenge your child to channel his energy into a better choice. When he does, he will feel better about his choice and about himself. This is why children get happier when they receive lovingly firm discipline. This is one of many ways that we know appropriate spankings do not have the negative effects some people say they do, because children who are disciplined in this way become happier.

At first, your child's battle against his impulses will still rage strong. He knows the sweet taste of getting his way sometimes, getting out of what he doesn't want, and getting the tons of hidden rewards he finds worthwhile. Your child will struggle to break these maladaptive patterns. Very firm consequences, that are not too hard but definitely not too soft, in the context of a loving relationship connect a "bitter taste" in your child's mind between the non-beneficial choice and the outcome. Your child will not connect in his heart the consequences with a bitter taste about his relationship with you. He will not because you have made sure first that your child knows that you love him and that anyone involved in the lovingly firm discipline loves him. Remember, it's not about whether the adult knows she loves the child. This is not enough. Your child has to know in his heart that the disciplinarian loves him. When he does, he is not confused about the consequences that you have told him would come for certain choices. Your child will make a direct connection between the non-beneficial choice and the lovingly firm consequences needed to help him push his energy into healthier choices.

Discipline cannot be equated to the proverbial "hot stove"— burn from a hot stove is so intense, we may only need to experience that once to be cautious forever. But there is no discipline that should equate to the pain of being burned by touching a hot stove, including appropriate lovingly firm spankings. Discipline must be consistent pain as needed—a pain that says, "I love you. I will not let you get away with this bad choice. I believe in your ability to do better, so in the most firm way I believe is fair, I will hold you accountable. I do not do this to harm you. I do this to help you see the importance of changing this behavior that is destroying you. I cannot make you change, but I also won't stand by and do nothing while you continue making choices that will kill your hopes, dreams and potential without you even knowing it." Spanking can be a powerful part of a discipline tool kit, along with other actions.

As I've already related in the companion book that goes with this guide, my kids will tell you that I employ very firm spankings, and they hurt. My kids cry, hurt, and still love me…thank God. I do not give spankings because I want to hurt them. I give spankings because sometimes that's what's needed to really help them think about the choice and think twice about making it. I know that sometimes spankings are the Most Effective way to get through to my children. The same might be true of you and your child. Even so, when we decide to spank and make it effective in the context of a loving relationship when our child crosses specific boundaries, we do not bring pain equivalent to a hot stove or anything close to that.

Our lovingly firm discipline will not be a one-and-done experience, so we must Persevere with love. No matter what discipline we use for our kids, there is something about the loving relationship that discipline can never equal. I shared in the book *I've Tried Everything* about a teen whose mom got so desperate for him to get up for school that she splashed him with water as he lay in bed, and on one occasion crawled onto the roof and through his window to wake him up when he locked his bedroom door. I'm not advocating the methods, but what I want you to know is what that teen told me in my office afterward. He said he finally decided to change and do what was needed to get up on his own and go to school every day not because of the water, the roof or any of his mother's other desperate efforts, but because "she never stopped loving me and I got tired of seeing her hurt."

No matter what you do, never stop chasing your child's heart. If you are so frustrated with your child that you can hardly be around him, accept it. Remember, you might even need to speak the truth in love with your child. "Sam, I love you, and I always will, but I don't like you right now. Your behavior drives me crazy, and I want to scream and run away. I won't though because I love you. Because I love you, I'm going to punish you. What did you do that I told you I will not tolerate? (The child answers). Right. You crossed that line. I know you are capable of controlling yourself. Here are your consequences."

Find your own way to try to love your child through your frustration. Know that loving your child means stepping up your game with discipline. It means loving your child enough to embrace the truth about spanking and doing it if you need to. Loving your child means spending time with them at times that make sense like dinner, being there for school and other important events or even that one minute of focused attention before bed. "How do kids spell love? T.I.M.E." – Zig Ziglar.

Our child's behavior dictates our response. One child may get spankings, a lot of them, while another might not. Embrace the truth with yourself and your children that you love each one enough to give them what each child needs individually. If a child breaks the family law, that child will be disciplined accordingly. That's the way of it. If one child breaks the law and the others do not, each child should receive the consequences appropriate to their actions. Remember the word *consequences* relates to appropriate outcomes of a choice, not just punishment. Don't feel guilty if one child spends the day watching TV and having fun while the other spends all day in his room with nothing but a book to read. Decide what's fair for each child and, to the best of your ability, respond accordingly.

Spanking appropriately is challenging. It takes as much skill to learn how to do this as it does to learn many other important endeavors in life. We have to learn how to spank in the Goldilocks zone, not too hard and not too soft. This takes work, effort and practice. As a caregiver, I've made mistakes in judgment and errors in discipline and so will you. The key is the heart. The key is to own mistakes, apologize for them and always learn from them. We must not let our mistakes cause us to be fueled with guilt that keeps us from learning and being the Most Effective we can be in parenting and disciplining our kids. I did not make mistakes as a parent to try to hurt my children. I made these mistakes because I'm human and a parent. It's impossible to avoid ever making a mistake.

The key is to put our child's best interest at the forefront. I cannot change the fact that some have and will beat children and say those beatings are for the child's best interest. These aggressive actions are not appropriate spankings; they are malevolent rage in disguise. I'm sorry for those of you that have endured a person in power taking their anger and aggression out on you.

As caregivers, our children need us to move past our fear, past our hurt, past our worry and past our refusal to embrace the truth about appropriate spankings when necessary. No matter how challenging, let us walk in truth about appropriate spanking from this point forward, together.

SPANKING: GUIDELINES AND TIPS

Caregivers who most often play the most active role in raising children today are female. Most female caregivers that have trouble spanking effectively are confused about what discipline is right for their child. They love their child and don't want their relationship with the child to suffer. They don't want their child's heart or spirit to be damaged in any way. Females usually do not have the problem of spanking too hard, which we know is unhelpful and abusive. Most caregivers today have the problem of being very inconsistent with spanking or not spanking hard enough—giving a spanking that is mostly due to frustration instead of a methodical part of healthy discipline. Also, many caregivers are being led by our medical system to believe their children cannot control their choices, causing the idea of spanking to seem inappropriate. I hope the information you have read in this *Resource Guide* and in the companion book *I've Tried Everything & Nothing Works* has helped you work through these concerns and challenged you to seek your Purpose for your child beyond the pain.

What is your Purpose for your child? What is your hope for your child? What does your child need to be empowered to redirect his energy into beneficial choices resulting in good feelings about himself? If you courageously decide your child may need appropriate spankings as part of his overall discipline package, you must spank effectively or not at all. In the 1997 film "Titanic," Jack—played by Leonardo DiCaprio—inspirationally talks about "making it count" as he discussed the way he pursued each day of his life. Making it count when it comes to spanking means doing it effectively. If you are going to spank, make it count.

Kids often don't take spankings seriously because they don't really hurt. Sure, kids are great about feigning pain. They scream, cry and wail, often before the spanking even begins. I've heard of many children talking, yelling, arguing, fussing and being angry with the parent during a spanking. If your child is doing any of the aforementioned behaviors during a spanking or if your child is crying but not truly because the spanking hurts, you are not spanking hard enough.

I'd say that caregivers who choose to spank do so effectively about thirty percent of the time on average. Many caregivers recognize their spankings probably truly hurt only about a third of the time, and this is after going through all the antics and world war three to get it done. Spankings just do not seem to be worth it.

Male caregivers more often have to guard against spanking too hard. A child's reaction is not the only indicator that a spanking is too hard—some children react out of proportion to the pain. It takes deliberate wisdom to give a healthy, appropriate spanking in the Goldilocks zone.

Also, the too hard or too soft lack of effectiveness is not always gender specific for caregivers. How well do you do at knowing the Goldilocks zone of spanking when it comes to your child? I can assure you that your child knows, and that child also likely believes deep down that effective spankings help him. Your child is just smart enough not to tell you he knows this.

The issue is not whether you do or don't spank; you get to decide that. If you are going to spank, though, you need to make it effective or don't do it at all. Try to make your decision about including spanking in your discipline tool belt not based on your feelings or other opinions but on the truth about appropriate spankings and the level of lovingly firm discipline that your child likely needs. For those of you who choose to make healthy, lovingly firm spankings an empowering aspect of your child's transformative process, I'm going to teach you how to make spankings effective.

How to Spank Appropriately and Effectively

Let's first establish unified nomenclature during this discussion. We will distinguish the difference among striking, swatting, and spanking.

Striking – Never Appropriate:

- Striking is any type of physical contact with a child motivated by or a reaction to feelings, even if done in the method of an appropriate spanking. We can be angry, but physical discipline must never be a *reaction* to anger.
- Striking is punching with a fist, slapping in the face or on the body, pushing (except away with appropriate force in self-defense), or kicking.
- Striking is hitting a child with any thrown object.
- Striking is popping a child in the mouth.

- Striking it hitting a child anywhere else on the body besides the bottom (or hand for very young children).
- Striking is using inappropriate objects and/or excessive force in physical discipline.
- Striking emotionally, which can be more damaging, is using negative words, even to try to motivate, including but not limited to name-calling, berating, cursing at or around, slamming or throwing objects around a child due to anger or frustration

Swatting – Appropriate and Healthy When Done Correctly:

- Swatting is a form of physical discipline for a young toddler over 15 months to about 2 to 3 years of age.
- Swatting is physically disciplining a young child by using your hand to hit the child on the hand one to three times to teach something like "don't touch."
- Swatting may include two or three firm swats on the buttocks, through clothing.

Spanking – Appropriate and Healthy When Done Correctly:

- Spanking is an intentional method of physical discipline for a toddler of 18 months up to about 12 years of age.
- Spankings are administered only on a child's bottom.
- An appropriate and effective spanking can be given with the hand, a wide belt or a paddle.

A spanking must have the following elements to be appropriate:

- Administered only by a person the child knows loves him
- Hard enough to truly hurt but not leave bruises or welts
- The caregiver must with the utmost care determine that their toddler/child is of an intellect, regardless of age, where it is clear

the choice they are making is intentional defiance and the child understands why they are receiving a spanking.

- Feeling angry when spanking is appropriate as long as the actions are in no way a reaction to the caregiver's feelings.
- Caregivers must maintain complete control of themselves and the situation.
- The spanking is handled according to the law governing the location where it takes place.

A spanking must have the following elements to be effective:

- About 2 to 3 spanks on the bottom for ages 18 months to 3 or 4 years of age
- About 3 or 4 spanks on the bottom for ages 4 to 6
- About 4 to 6 spanks on the bottom for ages 6 to 12; 7 spanks on the rare occasion when it is needed
- Diaper and pants on is okay for a toddler. For a 3 to 4 year old, a bare bottom hand spanking may be the most effective but underwear/pants on is okay as long as you are able to spank firmly enough with control to make the spanking effective. Underwear on but not pants, shorts, etc. for ages 4 to 12. For children 4 and older, underwear only if appropriate relationally. Pants on may be more appropriate based on a child's physical, mental and emotional development, gender and relational factors. Make sure your spanking is firm enough through the diaper, underwear or pants to truly hurt without going overboard.
- Must be in the Goldilocks zone for the particular child—not too hard and not too soft.

Truths About Appropriate Spankings

Let me share truths that I hope are helpful as you are endeavoring to discern whether spanking is appropriate for your child:

- When kids know they are loved and know why they are getting a firm spanking, they know deep down the spanking is about correcting the choice they made.
- If work takes up a lot of your time or if your child doesn't live with you, discipline only on the foundation of a healthy relationship. This doesn't mean being a "Disney" caregiver, but also be certain that you avoid your main interaction with your child being when they are in trouble.
- Spanking too hard is wrong and abusive.
- Most caregivers struggle with not spanking hard enough to make the spanking effective.
- If your child is talking to you, yelling at you, "fake crying," being dramatic, or acting mad at you during a spanking, you are likely not spanking hard enough.
- An effective spanking is always in the Goldilocks zone—not too hard and not too soft for that particular child.
- Effective spankings hurt. Your child will be crying not because they are upset or angry but because of true pain. If your child is not crying because of true pain, (or noticeably stunned for very young children), your spanking is ineffective.
- My guess is that most caregivers spank effectively less than 50% of the time they go through the act. For many, I believe effective spankings happen closer to a third of the time.
- Appropriate and effective spankings are very firm, yet do not leave welts or bruises on children. Depending on the child's complexion, transient discoloration of the skin can and will occur, such as redness. An area spanked firmly and effectively should never develop welts and never become bruised so that it turns green, black or blue.
- I find it important to check my child's bottom after a firm spanking. The situation and relationship should always be so that there is no question of the integrity of checking a child's bottom. Welts

or bruises indicate you unintentionally spanked too hard. Evaluate yourself honestly. Did you lose control at any point during spanking or did you make an unintentional mistake in the process of trying to give a firm and appropriate spanking? If you lost control, stop spanking altogether and get help. Do not resume spanking until you are absolutely certain you can exercise complete self-control while spanking effectively. If you know you unintentionally spanked too hard, do not stop spanking altogether; just adjust the intensity of your spanking to avoid it happening again. If you unintentionally leave a welt or a bruise a second time while spanking, regardless of time frame, stop spanking, get help and figure out how to resume without making mistakes. Unintentional mistakes are time for serious self-evaluation and hard work to be healthy and effective when spanking, not give up if your child could benefit from this tool of lovingly firm discipline. Spanking slightly too hard should be EXTREMELY RARE, but if it happens, apologize to your child. Be careful to specify that you are apologizing because you unintentionally spanked too hard, not because you spanked.

- Manage your own fear of spanking. Gain control of yourself. Just as anger should not compel you to spank, fear should not stop you from spanking. Spank in line with your Purpose for your child.

- Your children will experience pain in life while learning from the choices they make. Will that pain be from someone who loves them or from this world, who doesn't love them?

- Allow your child to fail today and hurt today from their non-beneficial choices in the hopes that a measured amount of pain today will save a lot of pain tomorrow.

- Spank or don't spank based on what you believe in for your child. Trust yourself and be effective, whether you spank or not.

- An effective spanking on the bottom generally requires 2 to 3 spanks for children 18 months to about 3 years old and 4 to 6 spanks sometimes, rarely, 7 for children 4 through 11 years old.

These numbers give an idea about how many spanks an effective spanking will typically involve; however, adjust according to wisdom.

- Children should never be punched, slapped, kicked, struck, demeaned, cursed at or around or called names (including words like lazy, good for nothing, etc.). Children should never see an adult take their anger out on something or someone else when upset. There is no appropriate discipline that involves these actions.

- A child may be physically kept at arm's length as a deliberate action of defense to keep an aggressive child at bay who is trying to harm you or someone else, but only with enough force to keep them off of you.

- Always check your motives. No physical act of aggression should ever be perpetrated against a minor. Spanking and physical discipline done appropriately is never a physical act of aggression. Spanking is a consequence to discourage future bad choices of the same kind, not a retaliation for past actions.

- Exercise extreme caution and wisdom if there are physical health complications like seizures, heart conditions, etc. Use sound judgment to assess whether spanking would endanger the child based on a health condition or not. Check with a physician you can trust who will give you the facts about your child medically, not judge you based on what you believe may be effective discipline options if appropriate. Sometimes, you may have to also seek out a wise mental health professional to help you evaluate.

- Many childhood behavior problems are being attributed to neurological or neuro-biochemical problems when, in reality, most childhood behavior problems are a mix of the child's inner motivations, temperament, unbridled emotions and impulses and maladaptive habits.

Spanking Appropriately & Effectively in More Detail

During an appropriate spanking, a child may squirm and move. You must deliberately deliver the spanks hard enough to hurt while avoiding hitting anywhere except on the bottom. It is normal for a spank to land slightly on the leg, back or side when your child moves unexpectedly at the last second. This can happen on occasion that we miss the bottom, but we must ensure this is the rare occasion and always adjust accordingly. Try to adjust during the spanking so as to not stop the spanking. Maintain self and situational control and do your best to adjust to hit only on the bottom. Do stop the spanking though if you cannot spank appropriately or effectively because your child is moving too much and you cannot confidently hit only on the bottom. We as caregivers should never be striking a child on their legs, back, or anywhere else because we are careless.

Something I learned in my own family is that kids will almost always give female caregivers the hardest time when it comes to discipline. Before my wife Jen passed away from cancer, I learned that our kids would lie on the bed when I gave them a very firm and appropriate spanking. Even though the spanking hurt, they would "take it," if you will. When Jen went to spank, even though her spankings were not as hard as mine, the kids would carry on like she was killing them. The kids, all between the ages of 6 and 11, would grab the belt, fall on the floor, and refuse to lie on their stomachs or accept their spanking. They employed a wide variety of antics that they never used with me because female caregivers usually have to work two to four times as hard as the typical man to receive the same level of respect.

Your child can take the full measure of a firm and appropriate spanking without all the antics. Just like anything else, you may have to train your child to accept a spanking. Training your child to accept lovingly firm discipline is like training your child to meet any other Expectation that you have for him. Set two to three specific actions your child must take such as:

1. Remove pants when appropriate (leaving underwear on always)

2. Lie across the bed in a position that is best suited for you to firmly spank only on the bottom

3. Not get up or try to grab the belt

Be concise, and consistent with your Expectation and hold your child to it. Yes, it will hurt, and children will squirm; but they can learn not to fight you during the spanking. Hold them accountable without trying to corral, fight, beg or plead with your child to accept the spanking he is due according to the choice he made. Communicate to your child that nothing else, save what is necessary, will occur until he accepts his consequence fully as he is supposed to. In other words, respect and responsibility come first. Accepting consequences is a function of respect and responsibility. Until your child accepts his consequences, he only gets to eat, sleep, go to school and do what is essential. All privileges are off the table.

Appropriate spankings will hurt your child's body. This hurt, done purposefully, effectively, in healthy ways and on the foundation of a healthy, loving bond will strengthen your child's heart, mind and spirit. We must have the courage and fortitude to endure the momentary, transient pain to operate based on our child's needs, in every way imaginable, verses our feelings or fears. Lovingly firm and appropriate spankings are part of a path of hope and love.

Learning How to Spank Effectively

Appropriate spankings are always only in the Goldilocks zone for your particular child. Many caregivers have found that spankings "don't work." Often, it's because the *way* the spanking is conducted is not effective. I have heard many caregivers scoff at themselves when thinking about whether their spankings hurt or not. If you are nervous about spanking, this is normal, okay, and probably good. We want and need to do it right, and that takes effort and practice. If you are going to spank effectively, you must give your child a firm spanking, making it hurt without going too far. Here are some tested, helpful methods to help you Plan to spank effectively.

1. Get a wide belt or paddle, or plan to use your hand. You need an instrument that will hurt without leaving welts or bruises. The hand usually works well for younger children and/or can be used effectively on older children by caregivers who are physically very strong. Many caregivers cannot put enough "oomph" into a hand spanking to make it effective for older kids. You don't need some revolutionary device to spank; just use your wisdom along with a wide belt or paddle.

2. Gauge how hard to spank before you spank. We must find that Goldilocks zone, not too hard and not too soft for our particular child. If you haven't spanked this particular child before, are using a new belt or paddle, or are out of practice with spanking, gauging before the spanking can be extremely important. Do you want a crazy but effective way to gauge how hard to spank your child? Grab your belt or paddle or even use your hand. Sit on the edge of your bed and "spank" yourself on your inner thigh. No, this is not a masochistic move circa "The Scarlet Letter." The tenderness of the flesh of your inner thigh is likely close to the tender flesh of your child's bottom. If you have a significantly high pain tolerance in general or possibly in the area of your inner thigh, be careful with this.

3. Determine the appropriate number of spanks before you begin. See the guidelines earlier in our discussion on spanking. You have to discern what number is most appropriate to be effective in the Goldilocks zone based on your child.

4. Hit the Goldilocks zone. Pun intended here. The first spank or two of an appropriate spanking should be about 75% to 80% of the pressure needed to make the spanking effective for your child. After those initial spanks, try to get to 90% to 100% of the appropriate amount of pressure with the rest of the spanking. Most of the spanks, say 2 out of 3 for younger kids and 3 out of 5 or 6 for older kids, should be in the 90% to 100% range of pressure in order to make the spanking effective.

5. Check your child's bottom soon after, but not right after, the spanking. Give yourself time to settle and your child time to cry and settle. Make sure you didn't unintentionally create a welt or bruise or discoloration (temporary redness excepted). If so, check your motives and follow the guidelines shared earlier. Also, if needed, another caregiver who is in an appropriate position to check can help with this to assure the spanking is being given correctly.

Important Considerations When Spanking Appropriately & Effectively

You are not an abuser just because you spank…even if you have been abused. That is not who you are or how you live. This is true even if you've struggled. You must overcome your fear, shame, blame, and guilt and learn how to spank effectively. A caregiver's decision concerning spanking needs to be based on what is most beneficial for the child in question. Even though the idea of physical discipline can seem barbaric, we caregivers cannot get so lost in the challenge of appropriate spankings that we ignore that it can be one of the most helpful methods of deterring our children from non-beneficial patterns of behavior, especially children operating with the strong-willed temperamental affinity. For some, appropriate spankings may be the missing piece in the measure of lovingly firm discipline needed to help your child succeed.

Hand spankings on the bottom for children or smacks on the hand with your hand for very young children don't have anything to do with the myths about kids fearing your touch. That stuff is nonsense because kids don't learn to be averse to our touch when they receive fair, firm and appropriate spankings by someone they know genuinely loves them. The real consideration about hand spanking is whether it can be effective. If an adult lashes out and strikes a child with the hand, yes, the child will fear this type of retaliation; however, that is not what appropriate spankings entail. For a two- to three-year-old, spanking with your hand, if you can apply it in the Goldilocks zone of being hard enough, would likely be best. That might even be true with a four-year-old. However, most children five and older will likely need spankings with a belt or paddle to cause enough discomfort to yield results. Know your strength, and use wisdom.

I have seen children who have never been abused or even witnessed abuse flinch when a loving adult who has never lashed out at the child raises a hand for a random reason. This is a normal reaction. Evaluate your motives, how you have disciplined, and your relationship with the child. If all are healthy, these flinches are normal reactions from a child, especially in the presence of a caregiver they know means business.

Be careful not to go overboard and be abusive, but also don't waste your time being "underboard" and ineffective. If we are going to spank, we must make it effective or we create a scenario that is actually counter-productive. Your child must feel physical pain if an appropriate spanking is going to be effective. I do not enjoy spanking my kids. I've even dreaded it. I've hoped and prayed they did not make the choice that clearly would elicit a spanking as I've explained to them ahead of time. When my children have made the choice, I've hated at times to follow through with spanking; but I've followed through. Follow through so your child will take you seriously. Follow through because you are focused on your Purpose beyond the pain. If we want our child to honor the boundaries of "no meanness," respect, responsibility, self-control, and how to treat other people well, an appropriate spanking will at times be the Most Effective measure of discipline.

It's important that our children always understand why they are being spanked. As far as when to spank, this depends greatly on the age and intellect of your child. Children under the age of four probably need to be spanked right away if they do something wrong. Children four and older can be spanked later on in the day, as long as you are sure they understand. An example can be a child who fails to meet their Expectation of Excellence in the morning before school or before the caregiver leaves for work or one who fails to meet it while the caregiver is away during the day. It is appropriate to spank the child later in the day as long as the connection can be made to specifically why the child is receiving the spanking.

Older children, say six or older, may be able to understand specifically why they are receiving the spanking the next day after the offense. A potential scenario may be when a child refuses to comply with their firm and appropriate spanking initially and are ready to comply later because you have held your child Accountable. Questions that may help guide you are: How smart is my child? How likely is it that my child can understand later what they did wrong earlier? How well have I reinforced my Expectation of Excellence with my child that they understand clearly when they have violated it? You can wait until the Most Effective and appropriate time to discipline or spank as long as your child understands.

Everything we do as caregivers is not enjoyable. What we do as caregivers must always be intentional based on the love we have for our children. We love them enough to give them the lovingly firm discipline we believe will be Most Effective in the process of correcting them. Remember, the purpose of lovingly firm discipline, including spankings, is not actually punishment for the past; it's encouragement for the future. It is an encouragement to consider their choices in the future and make better ones.

I also implore you to check your motives as well as your process. Only God knows your heart. Your actions towards your child must be pure if you are going to bring in physical discipline. Check your actions and motives with trusted, wise advisors if needed to ensure that what you are doing is truly for your child's well-being and not deep down really about you.

Help your 12 and under, concrete-thinking child make a direct connection between non-beneficial choices and your lovingly firm discipline. In this way, we caregivers act in place of our child's developing prefrontal cortex, helping them to make a strong connection between choices and consequences and encouraging them to choose wisely.

SELF-CONTROL

The battles our strong-willed children face internally come out in behavior that is difficult, confusing and frustrating to understand. I've heard countless caregivers report that it's like they have two different children. The Dr. Jekyll and Mr. Hyde or Bruce Banner and the Incredible Hulk are primary comparisons when the "switch flips." At the risk of sounding insane, a risk I venture frequently, it is absolutely likely that your child can control herself. We just have to motivate her to push forward that control instead of the maladaptive responses.

Children can be upset without tantrums. They can be frightened without outbursts. They can be angry without lashing out. Yes, children enact these behaviors when they have difficult experiences and emotions. We see these reactions often when children are reacting directly to trauma. Yes, there are many children who have been traumatized, and many of you are raising previously traumatized children. What you must discern now, in wisdom, is whether the trauma is actually at the core of their present concerns or is it something else?

Is your child primarily having behavior problems when they don't get their way or are faced with doing something they don't want to do? Does your child display the behavior problems in some areas of their lives but not others on a fairly consistent basis? These are just a couple of clues that indicate a child is reacting not to a past trauma but to current circumstances they deem unpleasant. In these cases, smart children, as your child likely is, find "reasons" to not do what they don't want and to try to get what they want. These "reasons" come out in the form of confusing behavior.

Many caregivers, when they really think about it, can discern on some level when their child is really struggling with something or when they are trying to get their way. Start with that and go from there. Challenge your child to choose healthy methods of dealing with their emotions and behavior. Give them healthy outlets to express their feelings and build relationships where they trust you to talk about their feelings. A great book for this is *How to Talk So Kids Will Listen and How To Listen So Kids Will Talk* by Adele Faber and Elaine Mazlish.

Life does not always present the perfect opportunity for us to address our emotions. Kids don't need the perfect opportunity. Each struggle with emotions is an opportunity for them to practice self-control. More than anything, we need to help our children practice self-control so they can choose the healthy outlets instead of letting their emotions get the best of them. This means understanding the appropriate time and place for everything.

A child may get angry in class when it's the appropriate time to maintain control and continue to do their work. This is best for a child to learn and strengthens them when we empower them accordingly. Children do not need to go out of class to quiet places to calm down. The real world does not work like this, and such practices diminish the truth of self-control. Self-control is a real and powerful thing. Due to the way children behave, we are led to believe they cannot control themselves. Most can. Even the ones with the "switch flipping," behavior. I know because I've seen countless "out of control" kids control themselves on a dime. When you look carefully, you may be able to discern times your child demonstrates the very control you want him to have. These are indications of the full nature of what your child is capable of.

The first element of your child's success is for you to believe your child can succeed. The words *capable* and *accountable* end in "able." If we do not have faith that our children are fully cap-able we will not hold them fully account-able. If we do not believe they are truly able and act accordingly, how can we expect change to occur? Odds are that it won't.

It can take great courage to believe children are capable of learning to control themselves and eliminate the behavior problems they have. This takes great courage because you do not want to hold your child to an Expectation that is beyond his ability. I totally understand that concern. The problem is that we are setting the bar too low, seeing children as defective and thus unwittingly selling our children short. Your child can develop healthy, consistent, empowering self-control and overcome his problems, but he cannot do so without you. Your child will likely not succeed without you having faith in him and in your Plan to help him succeed. Even if you are not sure, just give the L.E.A.P. process the full-steam-ahead college try for six months and see for yourself. Your child cannot succeed without the full measure of Affirming Accountability from you that he needs, which says, "I believe in you, and I'm going to act like it." In this, we communicate an Expectation of Excellence that we believe our child can meet and, with every fiber of our being, in Love, we hold them Accountable. Remain consistent and Persevere until you see self-control blossom in your child.

THANKS

Thank you for reading this Resource Guide. Use it with Godly wisdom to develop your comprehensive Plan for Affirming Accountability, trusting in God every step of the way. You and your child will succeed.

CPSIA information can be obtained
at www.ICGtesting.com
Printed in the USA
JSHW031913210222
23172JS00006B/160

9 781950 685844